T0317531

Profit and the Environment

TITLES IN THE UK SIP SERIES

BRANDS: VISIONS AND VALUES
Edited by John Goodchild and Clive Callow

FORTHCOMING TITLES IN THE UK SIP SERIES

FILM FINANCE
Bill Baillieu and John Goodchild

ASSET MANAGEMENT: EQUITIES DEMYSTIFIED
Shanta Acharya

SOCIALLY RESPONSIBLE INVESTMENT: A PRACTICAL GUIDE FOR
PROFESSIONAL INVESTORS
Russell Sparkes

Series Editors: John Goodchild and Clive Callow

Profit and the Environment
Common Sense or Contradiction?

Hilary Stone

and

John Washington-Smith

JOHN WILEY & SONS, LTD

Published in 2002 by John Wiley & Sons Ltd,
Baffins Lane, Chichester,
West Sussex P019 IUD, England
National 01243 779777
International (+44) 1243 779777

e-mail (for orders and customer service enquiries): cs-books@wiley.co.uk
Visit our Home Page on http://www.wiley.co.uk

Copyright © 2002 Hilary Stone and John Washington-Smith

Hilary Stone and John Washington-Smith have asserted their right under the Copyright, Designs and Patents Act 1988, to be identified as the authors of this work.

Other Wiley Editorial Offices

John Wiley & Sons, Inc., 605 Third Avenue,
New York, NY 10158-0012, USA

Wiley-VCH Verlag GmbH, Pappelallee 3,
D-69469 Weinheim, Germany

John Wiley & Sons Australia, Ltd, 33 Park Road, Milton,
Queensland 4064, Australia

John Wiley & Sons (Asia) Pte Ltd, 2 Clementi Loop #02-01,
Jin Xmg Distripark, Singapore 129809

John Wiley & Sons (Canada) Ltd, 22 Worcester Road,
Rexdale, Ontario M9W iLl, Canada

Library of Congress Cataloging-in-Publication Data
Stone, Hilary.
   Profit and the environment : commonsense or contradiction? / Hilary Stone
   and John Washington-Smith
      p. cm.
   ISBN 0-471-55945-8
   1. Industrial management–Environmental aspects. 2. Environmental policy.
   3. Profit–Moral and ethical aspects. 4. Pollution. I. Washington-Smith, John. II. Title.

   HD30.255.S767 2001
   333.7–dc21   2001045561

British Library Cataloguing in Publication Data
A catalogue record for this book is available from the British Library
ISBN 0-471-55945-8

Typeset in Rotis serif 10pt by Deerpark Publishing Services Ltd, Shannon, Ireland

Printed and bound by CPI Antony Rowe, Eastbourne

Contents

Contents

Contents

Acknowledgements

No publication is complete without acknowledgements and thanks, for no work of this type can be written in isolation. Ours are to the Institute of Risk Management and to John Arpel for their guidance in the risk issues we researched; to Morley Fund Management, Tomorrows Company and KPMG for answering all our questions in relation to socially responsible investment and related issues; to Robert Howard, FCA, of Crouch Chapman, Chartered Accountants, for reviewing the accountancy aspects of Chapter 4; to the OECD, the EU and the UK DEFRA for statistics and other information, and particularly to Paul Verstraete of the Belgium Ministerie van Middenstand en Landbouw for taking the trouble to translate statutes written in Flemish for us.

And finally to our respective spouses, Howard and Mary, without whose support this book would never have been written.

Abbreviations

AAA	American Accounting Association
ACBE	Advisory Committee on Business and the Environment
ACCA	Association of Chartered Certified Accountants
AQS	air quality standards
ASB	UK Accounting Standards Board
BAT	best available technologies/techniques
BPEO	best practicable environmental option
BSI	British Standards Institution
CA	competent authority
CBI	Confederation of British Industry
CEC	Commission of European Communities
CEN	Comité Européen de Normalisation (European Committee for Standardisation)
CERCLA	Comprehensive Environmental Response, Compensation, and Liability Act 1980 (US)
CHF	Swiss Francs
CFC	chlorofluorocarbon
CH_4	methane
CO	carbon monoxide
CO_2	carbon dioxide
COM	Commission of the European Communities
COP	Conference of the Parties
DEFRA	Department of the Environment, Food and Rural Affairs (superseded MAFF and DETR on 8 June 2001) (UK)
DETR	Department of the Environment, Transport and the Regions (UK)
DG	Directorate General of the European Commission
DTI	Department of Trade and Industry (UK)

DTLR	Department of Transport, Local Government and the Regions (superseded DETR on 8 June 2001) (UK)
EAA	European Accounting Association
EA	Environment Agency (England)
EC	European Community
EEA	European Environment Agency
EEC	European Economic Community
EIA	environmental impact assessment
EIRIS	Ethical Investment Research Service (UK)
EMAS	Environmental Management and Audit Scheme (EU)
EMS	environmental management system
EPA	Environmental Protection Agency (US)
ESM	environmentally sound management
EU	European Union
EWC	European Waste Catalogue
FASB	Financial Accounting Standards Board (US)
GAAP	generally accepted accounting standards (US)
GRI	Global Reporting Initiative
HCFC	hydrochlorofluorocarbon
HCl	hydrochloric acid
HFC	hydrofluorocarbon
HSE	Health and Safety Executive (UK)
IASC	International Accounting Standards Committee
ICC	International Chamber of Commerce
IISD	International Institute for Sustainable Development
IPCC	Intergovernmental Panel on Climate Change
IPPC	Integrated Pollution Protection Control (EU)
IRRC	Investor Responsibility Research Center
ISAR	Intergovernmental Working Group of Experts on International Standards of Accounting and Reporting of the United Nations
ISO	International Organisation for Standardisation
LAAPC	Local Authority Air Pollution Control (England)
LCA	life cycle assessment
NGO	non-governmental organisation
NIMBY	not in my backyard
N_2O	nitrous oxide

NO$_x$	nitrogen oxide
O$_3$	ozone
OECD	Organisation for Economic Cooperation and Development
PCB	polychlorinated biphenyl
PPP	polluter pays principle
RCRA	Resource Conservation and Recovery Act 1976 (US)
SEC	Securities and Exchange Commission (US)
SME	small or medium-sized enterprise
SO$_2$	sulphur dioxide
TAR	third assessment report
TQM	total quality management
UN	United Nations
UNCED	United Nations Conference on Environment and Development
UNEP	United Nations Environment Programme
VOC	volatile organic compound
WTO	World Trade Organisation

A Brief Introduction to the Environment

Why the compulsion to write another book about the environment? Because the end of the twentieth century was marked by pessimism concerning mankind's impact on the environment and some optimism that the new millennium would see consensus on the causes of the planet's environmental problems and agreement on the solutions to them. One area of consensus is that the relationship between mankind and his environment is complex and that any solution to the problem needs to consider not only environmental factors, but social and economic or business issues too. This book focuses on how business is reacting to the environmental challenge, and finds hope for the future.

However, in this far from ideal world, attitudes to the environment demonstrate both a lack of ideology and by contrast an excess of ideology. This book seeks to identify those contrasts. On the one side those who disregard the environment entirely, on the other, those who seek to extend the cutting edge of environmental thinking. There are new trends and this book seeks to identify them. A look is taken at current approaches to environmental reporting and accounting, the reasons why ethical and social investing (in an environmental context) are coming to the fore, the impact of new trends in risk management, how from these issues and others it is possible to identify a strong performer and why the environment coupled with sustainable development seems set to become even more significant.

The word 'environment' appears overworked. A dictionary definition assists in putting the word and the subject into context. According to the Shorter Oxford English Dictionary (1980 edition), the first use of the word 'environment' was in 1603, meaning 'the action of environing' or 'forming a ring around, surrounding or encircling' – and that is no bad definition for 2001. We are encircled by everything we emit into the air, deposit onto the land and discharge into the water. It follows that it is not only the environment that may suffer from our emissions, deposits and discharges but also that there are social implications of our conduct that must be addressed.

However, from the devising of that first definition in 1603 and for the next nearly two hundred years, we lived more or less in harmony with our environment. This is not to say that there are no early examples of environmental legislation. Both air and water pollution were identified as problems hundreds of years ago in the UK. As to water, with the passing into law in 1388 of an act forbidding the dumping of animal remains, dung and garbage into rivers, ditches and streams, because of the 'great annoyance, damage and peril of the inhabitants' and as to air, when the use of coal was banned in London in 1273, as being prejudicial to health. It must be said, however, that the act was more honoured in the breach than in the observance because there are also later examples of similar legislation and tracts and papers condemning the quality of the air linked to use of coal, written by aggrieved citizens throughout the centuries.

And then came the Industrial Revolution. For a while the UK struggled with the consequences of unregulated pollution, but by the middle of the nineteenth century it was using the concept of 'best practicable means' to underpin its approach to pollution control, and by the beginning of the twentieth century, government had worked out a schedule of polluting processes and linked it to a list of noxious and offensive gases.

It was with this type of legislation in place that industry proceeded through the early part of the twentieth century. New processes caused new and different pollutants to escape, and legislators struggled to catch up and regulate after the event. And all of this was against a background of the increasing need to allow free development of trade and industry, at almost whatever the cost.

The UK was not alone in the headlong dash for industrialisation, it was happening all over the First World at approximately the same time. Increasingly, however, it came to be seen that all was not well with the environment. Environmental damage was being suffered which could not easily be repaired. It seemed too difficult a task for any one country to handle on its own, but one of the beneficial effects of two world wars was to bring the nations of the world closer together, first under the auspices of the League of Nations and then of the United Nations.

Governments started to discuss environmental issues, one with the other, and at national as well as international forums there was a growing recognition that something had to be done. The United Nations Environment Programme was formed as an arm of the United Nations, tasked among other things with pioneering the development of international environmental law. So it was that in Stockholm in 1972 the United Nations Conference on the Human Environment considered the need for a common outlook and for common principles to inspire and guide the peoples of the world in the preservation and enhancement of the human environment, and proclaimed that 'Man is both creature and moulder of his environment, ... a stage has been reached when, through the rapid acceleration of science and technology, man has acquired the power to transform his environment in countless ways and on an unprecedented scale.'

And thus it came to be seen that to preserve the precious natural resources still left to the world, international intervention was little short of mandatory. Over the next twenty years came UN conventions such as those to combat desertification, to protect the ozone layer and to regulate transboundary movement of hazardous wastes, all designed to assist in the implementation of the proclamations of the 1972 Stockholm Declaration. And, of course, it was in the latter part of this period that the General Agreement on Tariffs and Trade (GATT) – now the World Trade Organisation (WTO) – perceived the need for a standard to which businesses interested in the environment could work. The International Organisation for Standardisation (ISO) became involved and ISO 14001 (the standard governing environmental management systems) was published in 1996.[1]

[1] ISO is a worldwide federation of national standards bodies from some 130 countries, one from each country. Founded in 1947 it is non-governmental. The mission of ISO is 'to promote the development of standardization and related activities in the world with a view to facilitating the international exchange of goods and services, and to developing cooperation in the spheres of intellectual, scientific, technological and economic activity'. ISO is not an acronym, it is a word derived from the Greek *isos* 'equal'. From 'equal' to 'standard' was the line of thinking that led to the choice of the name ISO. Moreover, because it is not an acronym, it followed that the term could be used in every country, however the name was translated.

These international initiatives struck a resonant chord with those operating at national level. For example, in the United States by the end of the 1960s, pressure groups were taking seriously the adverse environmental impacts of industrialisation. Environmental issues moved from being of marginal interest, to the top of the public and political agenda. US environmental laws became stricter and then more stringently enforced. Penalties and financial liabilities, which had formerly been ignored as insignificant in comparison with the scale of corporate activity, began to become a matter of corporate concern. Industrial producers soon became aware of the impact of environmental consumerism and this added to the impetus for companies to address environmental issues as a management priority.

The first range of 'green' products such as washing powder and bleach became available in the 1980s but US citizens and their European counterparts proved not to be gullible and required green claims to be substantiated. This led to a plethora of eco-labels, systems for labelling products to demonstrate that they complied with environmental criteria. The Blue Angel scheme operating in Germany became well known and well recognised, leading to adoption of a scheme by the European Union. Implementation of the scheme has had its ups and downs, and this serves to demonstrate the struggle that resulted from the needs of environmental imperatives on the one hand and the requirements of business on the other.

The recognition of the need for stricter environmental regulation was reflected too in the work programme of the European Union (or European Economic Community as it then was) At the outset, Europe followed the United States mindlessly, if slowly. What occurred from an environmental standpoint in the US in the 1970s and 1980s happened in Europe ten years later. Public concern was expressed volubly over spills by ICI, over Shell's expressed intention (never carried out) to dump an oil platform in the North Sea, and as in the US over supermarkets, which made claims for 'green' products which did not bear much scrutiny. A valuable lesson was learned: not many consumers will pay enhanced prices for everyday products, even when the green credentials are impeccable. And this, as will be seen, is reflected in the fact that when faced with the choice of investing in a fund whose green credentials are sound or investing in a fund for maximum profit, most investors will select the latter while recognising that profit should not be the only driver.

That acknowledged, most would also accept that there are presently three critical environmental issues:

- Climate change: whether or not change will occur irrespective of how the planet is treated
- Pollution: its reduction and its impact on the environment
- Sustainable development: the cornerstone of the European view of environmental policy and increasingly, the United States

Somehow it is necessary to reconcile wealth creation with environmental care. Once that key challenge is successfully completed, the pursuit of sustainable development will be that much closer to accomplishment, and with the attainment of sustainability there will be an inevitable converging of the lines representing social impact, environmental impact and the financial stability of business.

Most of the topics covered in this book are developing rapidly. For example, the FTSE4Good indices were launched after our manuscript had been delivered to the publishers. The materials and description are intended to be generally complete up to April 2001. However, thanks to our publisher's tolerance we have been able to include some major items occurring later in 2001.

PART 1

A Changing World

CHAPTER 1

The Environment

INTRODUCTION

The latter half of the twentieth century witnessed a period of unprecedented economic growth and prosperity, at least in the developed world. The 1990s, in particular, saw the Dow Jones Industrial Average (Dow Jones Industrial Index, http://averages.dowjones.com/home.html) reach new highs, rising from about 3,000 in 1990 to over 11,000 by the end of the decade. Although much of the euphoria surrounding the world economy's seemingly limitless capacity for growth had evaporated by the turn of the millennium, the International Monetary Fund's forecast for the immediate future remained optimistic (IMF World Economic Outlook, www.imf.org/external/pubs/ft/weo/2000/02/index.htm). In October 2000 it projected that global real gross domestic product (GDP) for that year would be the strongest in over a decade. Moreover, it would remain at high levels during 2001 due in part to the remarkable strength of the US economy, supported by a robust expansion in Europe and the countries in transition. How quickly events such as those of 11th September 2001, can impact on the international economy.

It is easy to celebrate the technological triumphs that have underpinned mankind's material progress and to overlook the environmental cost that is beginning to be only too apparent. Quite simply, it is becoming increasingly difficult to disguise the fact that mankind's progress has been at the expense of the finite resources that are essential to his well-being. Mankind evolved to his present physical and cerebral state as a hunter-gatherer in harmony with his environment. As such, nature placed strict limits on man's potential for affecting his environment. Typically, then as

3

now, once a band of hunter-gatherers had exhausted the local supply of animal prey or in-season fruits, they were forced to move on. In time, the local population of prey species would recover and the seasons would see to it that fruits and the like would reappear in due course. Thus, putting aside natural catastrophes, hunter-gatherer groups could circulate within their territories with a reasonable expectation that their essential demands would be met by natural cycles of regeneration. On the other hand, when local populations outgrew their local environment, migration to less densely populated areas might be an option.

Now, only a few isolated tribes who have become objects of curiosity follow the way of the hunter-gatherer. However, while most observers note the contrasts between the hunter-gatherers' way of life and that of the rest of the world, there is one fundamental similarity: each is dependent on the finite resources provided by the Earth's natural systems.

Business fully understands the relationship between monetary 'capital' and 'income'; however, the same cannot be said of its relationship with the environment. The environment, too, can be described as 'capital'; after all, it is a limited resource from which a finite 'income' can be derived. Unfortunately, the evidence for strategic short-sightedness in this respect is emerging all around. Examples include climate change, water pollution and falling water tables, shrinking forests, eroding soils, depleted fish stocks, contaminated land, and disappearing plant and animal species.

This chapter briefly examines some of these issues, starting with arguably the most significant, climate change. It also examines the role played by population growth in forcing environmental damage, before concluding with a brief examination of the concept of sustainable development and its likely impact on strategic business thinking.

CLIMATE CHANGE

What is climate?

In discussing climate change, it is important to distinguish between climate and weather. Climate is the average weather, including seasonal extremes and variations, locally, regionally or globally. Weather can vary rapidly from day to day and from year to year under the influence of local temperature changes, winds, precipitation and clouds. Climate, however, changes only slowly under the influence of features such as the oceans and the energy released by the sun. Put simply, climate is controlled by the Earth's atmosphere, which balances the absorption and reflection of energy emitted by the sun. Most radiated energy from the sun is absorbed at the Earth's surface and in the surrounding atmosphere. Much of this energy is then radiated into space in the form of infrared, or heat, radiation. However, the so-called greenhouse gases, among which are carbon dioxide, methane, water and nitrous oxide, trap some radiated heat in the lower part of the Earth's atmosphere. This is the greenhouse effect; without it, the average surface temperature would be about 34°C (61°F) colder than it is today.

The delicate balance between absorbed and radiated energy can be disturbed by natural events. Significant volcanic eruptions can project dust particles into the atmosphere and these can block sunlight and lower surface temperatures for years at a time. Variations in ocean currents, too, can change heat and precipitation distribution. Perhaps the best-known of these phenomena is El Niño, in which there is a periodic warming of the central and eastern Pacific Ocean. Typically lasting between one and two years, El Niño events affect weather around the world, causing heavy rains in some places and droughts in others. However, nature is not the only influence at work on the atmosphere.

In its Second Assessment Report, published in 1996, the Intergovernmental Panel on Climate Change (IPCC) concluded that 'the balance of evidence suggests a discernible human influence on global climate'.[1] That said, it added the caveat that this evidence was 'still emerging from the background of natural climate variability'. The IPCC view is not universally accepted, though. There is a vociferous opposing camp which argues that recent evidence derived

[1] The IPCC is co-sponsored by the United Nations Environmental Programme and the World Meteorological Organisation, and it comprises 2,000 scientific and technical experts from around the world. It has so far published three assessment reports in 1990, 1996 and 2001. These are probably the most comprehensive and scientifically authoritative accounts of climate change.

from satellite data suggests that increased solar activity has been underestimated.

However, in its Third Assessment Report (TAR), published in 2001, the IPCC was able to state that, despite remaining uncertainties, there was 'new and stronger evidence that most of the warming observed over the last 50 years was attributable to human activities'. The report also concluded that most of the observed warming over the last fifty years was likely[2] to have been due to an increase in greenhouse gas concentrations. That said, the TAR could not completely account for changes in the atmosphere. The main uncertainty, which has long been used by climate change sceptics to undermine the credibility of global climate change models, was an inability to explain why satellite measurements since 1979 show that the global average temperature of the lowest 8 kilometres of the atmosphere has increased at a lower rate than the average surface temperatures.

The contribution of human activities to climate change

Prior to the Industrial Revolution, mankind's impact on the global climate was insignificant. However, during the industrial era, the intensive burning of fossil fuels such as coal, natural gas and oil, together with changes to land use, industrial processes and modern agricultural practices, has been altering the composition of the atmosphere and contributing to climate change. The IPCC reports that the concentration of carbon dioxide in the atmosphere has increased by 31% since the start of the industrial era. Furthermore, it claims that the present concentration of carbon dioxide has not been exceeded in the past 420,000 years and has probably not been exceeded during the past 20 million years. The IPCC estimates that the use of fossil fuels accounts for about 75% of the carbon dioxide currently being added by mankind to the atmosphere.

Changes to land use due to logging, ranching and agriculture also contribute to carbon dioxide emissions. Although dead or burnt vegetation releases carbon dioxide, natural regrowth absorbs carbon dioxide and ensures that the net emission is zero or minimal. With land clearance, however, net carbon dioxide emissions are

[2] The IPCC defines 'likely' as a 66–90% chance.

significant, as there is relatively little regrowth. On a more positive note, it seems that reforestation in the northern hemisphere is beginning to redress this balance to a small extent although, over-all, land changes are still responsible for 15–20% of current carbon dioxide emissions.

The IPCC reports that emissions of other greenhouse gases continue to rise, too. For example, concentrations of methane have risen by 151% during the industrial era. Just over half of methane emissions are the result of human activities such as use of fossil fuels, cattle, rice agriculture and landfills. During the same period, concentrations of nitrous oxide have risen by 17% and continue to increase. About a third of current nitrous oxide emissions originate with human activity.

Rising temperature
According to the IPCC's TAR, the Earth's surface warmed by 0.6±0.2°C during the twentieth century. However, the global rate of change may have increased during the 1990s, which was probably the warmest decade since recording began in 1861. The TAR also concludes that analysis of proxy data (e.g. from tree rings and ice core samples) indicates it is likely that the 1990s was the warmest decade in the northern hemisphere for the last 1,000 years. Less is known about annual averages for the previous 1,000 years and for most of the southern hemisphere prior to 1861. Other evidence for warming during the twentieth century includes a rise in sea levels of between 10 and 20 centimetres, the shrinkage of mountain glaciers, a reduction in northern hemisphere snow cover, and increasing subsurface ground temperatures (witness the appearance of mammoth carcasses in Russia from ground previously frozen for thousands of years).

There are several complementary pieces of evidence that point to mankind as the source of recent changes in carbon dioxide levels. First, scientists have been measuring total carbon dioxide levels for the past fifty years and their data reveals that global carbon dioxide levels have been rising steadily throughout this period.

Secondly, it is known that the nuclei of carbon atoms emitted by the burning of fossil fuels such as coal, oil and natural gas differ from those of carbon atoms in carbon dioxide emitted naturally. Fossil fuels were formed millions of years ago and as a result the fraction of their nuclei that was once radioactive has long since decayed to become non-radioactive carbon. On the other hand, carbon dioxide emitted to the atmosphere from natural sources (e.g. decaying vegetation) contains a portion of radioactive carbon. This is the dominant fraction of carbon in the atmosphere prior to the industrial era. However, since then the burning of fossil fuels has emitted non-radioactive carbon, thus reducing the proportion of radioactive carbon dioxide present in the atmosphere. There is similar evidence to be evinced from carbon dioxide captured within tree rings.

The third piece of evidence is supplied by bubbles of air trapped in samples of ice taken from the Antarctic ice caps and Greenland. Carbon dioxide concentrations present in shallow ice samples, which were laid down in the past few decades, were consistent with concentrations present in the atmosphere when the ice was formed. However, the concentration of carbon dioxide within deep, and therefore older, ice was 25% less than in the shallow samples. Significantly, concentrations in the deeper samples remained almost constant for a period of 10,000 years before the industrial era and the subsequent intensive use of fossil fuels.

Predictions for climate change

The IPCC currently forecasts that global average temperatures will further increase by between 1.4 and 5.8°C over the period 1990 to 2100. The range of estimated warming takes account of different emissions scenarios and varying assumptions about the sensitivity of the global climate to the changes induced by greenhouse gases. Also, it is not possible to be precise about how other important factors such as future population growth, changes to land use and use of alternative energy sources will affect warming. Temperature changes will vary considerably from region to region and could occur gradually or suddenly in different regions. Over the same period, rising average temperatures will heat seawater, which will expand and cause sea levels to rise by between 9 and 88 cm. Melting of glaciers and ice caps will also contribute to rises in sea level. Populations in Bangladesh, parts of coastal China and Egypt will be particularly exposed.

The IPCC predicts other changes in weather and climate with some confidence. It is very likely[3] that there will be higher maximum temperatures and more hot days over nearly all land areas. Conversely, there will be higher minimum temperatures, fewer cold days and frost days over nearly all land areas. An increased risk of drought is likely in most mid-latitude continental interior locations, e.g. in most of North America, nearly all of Europe and parts of South America; however, periods of heavy rain are also very likely over many areas. There are also likely to be regional changes in crop yields and an enhanced possibility of famine in tropical, subtropical, semi-arid and arid locations.

In many countries, fresh water is already a scarce resource due to competing demands for water for industrial, drinking, washing and irrigation purposes. Climate change is likely to make matters worse and make water a source of friction and perhaps conflict in many regions.

Climate change may also have an adverse affect on human health. There is a risk that the range of organisms that transmit diseases such as malaria, dengue fever and yellow fever will extend to cover parts of the United States, Europe and Asia. Worst-case projections indicate that the zone of potential malaria transmission may enlarge from an area which currently contains about 45% of the world's population to one containing about 60% by the end of the twenty-first century.

POPULATION GROWTH

When considering the matters that truly impact on the planet, alongside climate change, population growth is the other significant threat to economic progress. The world population did not reach one billion until 1804 (United Nations, *The World at Six Billion*, www.un.org/esa/population/sixbillion.htm). It took 123 years to reach 2 billion in 1927, 33 years to reach 3 billion in 1960, 15 years to reach 4 billion in 1974, and 13 years to reach 5 billion in 1987. In 1999 it reached 6 billion. Currently, and despite falling birth rates, world population is projected to achieve 7 billion in 2013, 8 billion in 2028 and 9 billion in 2054 before stabilising at 10 billion in 2200.

[3] The IPCC defines 'very likely' as a 90–99% chance.

But other population changes are happening, too. The world has become increasingly urban. Between 1990 and 2025 the number of people living in urban areas is projected to be more than 5 billion, which will account for two-thirds of the world's population. Reflecting the move from rural to urban living, the number of megacities (defined as cities with a population greater than 8 million) rose from 2 in 1950 to 23 in 1995. By 2015 projections suggest there may be as many as 36 megacities, 23 of which will be located in Asia (World Resource Institute, www.wri.org/trends/citygrow.html, 23 February 2001).

Although, on the face of it, not an environmental problem, there is little doubt that population growth will expose mankind's disregard for the environment much earlier than might otherwise have been the case. Many developing countries already have urban centres that are overpopulated by most measures, and because these centres of overpopulation are to be found in undeveloped or developing countries, the problem is magnified by attendant problems of insufficient food supplies, deforestation to provide fuel for cooking what there is, lack of adequate fresh water, and inadequate infrastructure to deal with natural disasters when they strike (e.g. floods and earthquakes).

WATER RESOURCES

Another pressing environmental issue is that of freshwater supplies. Global water consumption rose fourfold between 1940 and 1990 and it continues to grow rapidly in response to increasing demands (World Resource Institute, www.wri.org/trends/water2.html, 21 February 2001). Agriculture currently demands 70% of available freshwater for irrigation, although the United Nations expects a further 50–100% increase in the need for irrigation water by 2025. Much of this will be required in developing countries, where population growth and the need for agricultural expansion will be greatest.

While freshwater is abundant globally, its distribution is very uneven and so local shortages often occur. Local or regional scarcity is often compounded by pollution, which reduces the available supply. In the developed world, extensive legislation and strict enforcement, together with major investment in water and sanitation infrastructure, are reducing this problem. However, even in the southern member states of the European Union, about 50% of the population are not connected to sewage treatment facilities. Meanwhile, freshwater pollution remains a major problem in Central Europe and Russia. The situation is much worse in developing states undergoing industrialisation and urbanisation, where water supplies are often poor and sanitation services minimal. Here the lack of legislation, enforcement and investment has exposed scarce water supplies to the full range of modern pollution problems, including heavy-metal pollution, eutrophication, acidification and persistent organic compounds.

Another recent problem concerning water is the depletion of water resources held in aquifers. Until the latter half of the twentieth century, consumption of this resource was limited by the capacity of pumping machinery. However, with the advent of large-capacity diesel and electric pumps, aquifers have been consumed at rates that exceed natural rates of replenishment. Examples of this are to be found in the Ogallala aquifer in the United States and in similar aquifers in North Africa, the Middle East, Southeast Asia and India.

Looking to the near future, by 2025 it is estimated that up to 1.8 billion people will experience absolute water scarcity (International Water Institute, Projected Water Scarcity 2025, www.cgiar.org/iwmi/home/wsmap.htm#A1). They will not have the means to maintain their current level of food production from irrigated agriculture as well as meeting their industrial and domestic water requirements. This could result in their becoming increasingly dependent on imported food, should they be able to afford it. Most countries in North Africa and the Middle East experience water scarcity today; by 2025 they will be joined by South Africa, China, Pakistan and large parts of India.

DISAPPEARING FORESTS

Until comparatively recently, most forest loss occurred in Europe, North Africa, the Middle East and temperate North America. By the early twentieth century these regions had lost much of their forest cover. In the past 30–40 years the attention of the timber industry has focused mainly on the tropics. Between 1960 and 1990 Asia lost one-third of its cover and Africa and Latin America lost 18% each.

Overall, this amounted to the loss of one-fifth of all tropical forest cover (*State of the World*, L. R. Brown, C. Flavin and H. French, Earthscan). Besides the need for timber and paper, there are several other reasons for deforestation (World Resource Institute, www.wri.org/trends/deforest/ html). In Africa and Asia the most common cause is the extension of subsistence farming, while in Latin America it is government-backed conversion of forest to other land uses such as large-scale ranching. Deforestation can affect watershed management, too. In 1998 the Chinese government acknowledged that the near-record flooding of the Yangtze river basin was exacerbated by the deforestation of the upper reaches of the watershed (*State of the World*, L. R. Brown, C. Flavin and H. French, Earthscan).

But the state of the world's forests cannot be expressed only in terms of hectares of coverage lost. Attention must also be focused on the health, genetic diversity and age profile of forests – collectively known as forest quality. In the developed countries, trees are being damaged by fire, drought, pests and air pollution, particularly acid rain. The seriousness of this problem is evident from a 1995 survey which recorded that 25% of trees assessed exhibited signs of defoliation. Another survey showed that the number of completely healthy trees fell from 69% of those examined in 1988 to 39% in 1995.

Continued forest loss and damage will have serious implications at local, regional and global levels. Not only is deforestation destroying the way of life for tens of thousands of indigenous peoples, it is significantly affecting biological diversity (often before the nature and extent of local flora and fauna are fully understood) and nutrient recycling, watershed management and climate regulation.

DEPLETION OF FISH STOCKS

Overfishing was recognised as an international problem in the early 1900s (World Resource Institute, www.wri.org/trends/fishloss.html, 21 February 2001). But before the 1950s, the problem was confined to relatively few regions such as the North Atlantic, the North Pacific and the Mediterranean. Now, according to the Food and Agriculture Organisation (FAO) of the United Nations, 35% of most important commercial fish stocks exhibit patterns of declining yields and require immediate action to halt overharvesting. The yields of a further 25% are steady; however, they are being fished at their biological limit and will be vulnerable to decline if fishing levels are increased. Significantly, the FAO notes that the harvest of over-exploited fish stocks declined from 14 million tonnes in 1985 to 8 million tonnes in 1994. Although not apparent from these figures, certain fish stocks, such as the Atlantic cod and haddock, have almost collapsed in some areas of the North Atlantic.

Fish are an important source of protein for mankind. They provide about one-fifth of animal protein in the human diet and about 1 billion people rely on them as their primary protein source. Indeed, global production of fish products exceeds that of poultry, beef or pork combined. Currently, the FAO estimates that some 80 million tonnes of fish are consumed annually but that demand is likely to climb to 110–120 million tonnes by 2010, in line with predictions for world population growth. However, only the most optimistic forecasts suggest that global fish stocks could service this demand.

INDUSTRIAL POLLUTION

Contaminated land

No overview of mankind's position at the beginning of the third millennium can be complete without reference to industrial pollution. This chapter has already touched on the adverse affects on water, forests, climate and fish of man's actions, but other areas too are distorted by man. Land is in finite supply on the planet. It may become contaminated as a result of a variety of human activities and the polluted soil may cause problems for centuries. Mining is well known for causing soil contamination, particularly mining of metal ores. The hazardous effects of spoil from Roman lead and silver mines may still be seen in parts of North Wales, while there is evidence of increased levels of cadmium in soil and vegetables in some parts of Somerset, resulting from zinc extraction. The effects of war on the environment are not the subject of this book but suffice it to say that depleted uranium, whenever and wherever used, will remain in the earth for hundreds of years and the effects of cluster bombs (the alternative to landmines) should not be underestimated.

Contamination of the soil with toxic chemicals, whether or not as a result of an industrial process, can directly impact on human health if the land is then used for housing without the necessary remediation being carried out. The chemicals can be ingested as particles by children playing, in fruit and vegetables if home-grown, or inhaled as dust or vapour. There are several different opportunities for pollutants once they reach the soil: they may break down or be neutralised; they may be washed out by rain; they may evaporate if volatile; or they may remain in the soil, accumulating over time until dangerous levels are present. What happens to pollutants, in terms of quantity and concentration, depends on the balance between their arrival and removal. Removal depends on the chemical, physical and biological properties of the contaminants and the soil medium, together with the presence and activity of soil organisms, rainfall and its composition, and the effect on the original pollutants of other contaminants that are subsequently added.

The total restoration of contaminated land to an unpolluted state is seldom achievable and seldom necessary. A remedial approach is often acceptable, tailored to the intensity and extent of the contamination, and the present and future uses of the land. Lightly contaminated land may perhaps be used for amenity purposes if the contaminants are largely inorganic and it is possible to plant tolerant grasses to act as an insulating layer between soil and humans. But if the land is heavily polluted then it may be that the only remedy is a concrete or tarmac cap and the use of the land for warehousing, car parking or some other similar use. There are several remediation processes, including solidification, physical treatment, chemical treatment, thermal treatment, and biological methods.

Waste

Of all the environmental issues, waste is one of the most difficult. It is produced, in our throwaway society, at home, at work and at leisure. It is sent down the drain, out the gate, up the chimney or buried. It is extremely difficult to estimate the total amounts of waste produced, whether in the UK, the EU, the US or the world. EU statistics indicate that 2000 million metric tonnes of waste are produced each year, of which 40 million tonnes are classified as hazardous. In the United

States the Office of Solid Wastes indicates that 220 million US tons of solid waste are produced each year and, in addition, 40 million US tons of hazardous wastes (to be fair, these figures relate only to solid wastes). Compare this figure with that offered by the EPA (see page 53). This disparity of figures indicates how difficult it is to obtain comparable statistics and how unreliable every set is – unless of course it is accompanied by a clear definition of what constitutes 'waste', for the purpose. The UK government itself in its document *A Way with Waste* - a draft waste strategy for England and Wales, June 1999, DETR; now replaced by *Waste Strategy 2000* - for England and Wales, May 2000, DETR, quoted more than one statistic for the same type of waste. Suffice it to say therefore that, world over, billions of tonnes of material must be recovered, recycled reused or disposed of each year. And this is part of the problem: the international community has chosen to define as 'waste' materials that are valuable and that are recoverable. Those materials must therefore be handled, treated, stored and disposed of as waste and are subject to waste regulation. Contrast this with product, most of which will end up as waste, to which no such panoply of strict regulation attaches.

Reducing the waste we produce is one of the challenges now facing us. It is not sensible to take our depleted resources and abandon them, when with some effort the waste need not be produced at all, or having been produced could be more sensibly utilised rather than abandoned. Moreover, the links between the disposal or emission of the by-products of industrial production and environmental damage are fundamental. Waste and environmental degradation may be viewed as synonymous. The challenge to industry as set out by mounting social and environmental pressures and ever more stringent legislation is to minimise its impact on the environment through changes in its products and how they are produced. At all stages the design of products and processes must incorporate the environmental perspective and work towards the goal of waste minimisation.

The by-products of production which constitute waste can take many forms, whether as gaseous, liquid or solid waste, but they have a wider dimension than the tangible measures of waste that are normally reported. It is not only the losses of materials and energy occurring as a result of production and use that constitute waste, but also the waste arising through the inefficient use of materials and energy. If there can be increases in efficiency and associated decreases in waste output then industry will minimise its environmental impact and improve its profitability. Waste is not only an environmental problem but a significant business problem. Whether due to the inherent underutilisation of resources or the non-optimal exploitation of raw materials, savings can be achieved that improve the bottom line and aid the environment. Effective waste management not only avoids significant input and disposal costs and liabilities, but through the creation of new market opportunities it can offer notable revenue-generating potential. Approaches to waste management are therefore of considerable importance to the continuing viability of both business and the environment, and a core requirement of sustainable development.

SUSTAINABLE DEVELOPMENT

In 1962 Rachel Carson wrote *Silent Spring*. Her book envisioned a world without environmental merit caused by man's flagrant disregard for his environment. It served as a wake-up call for many, as it was seen, perhaps for the first time, that there was a connection between the environment, the economy and social well-being. Directly from it, according to the US Environmental Protection Agency, came the National Environmental Protection Act 1969, and according to the International Institute for Sustainable Development (IISD), this was the catalyst that led indirectly to the UN Conference on Human Environment 1972 and therefore to the creation of the United Nations Environment Programme.

From this beginning came the increasing recognition that a balance had to be struck between protection of the environment on the one hand and more food and greater enjoyment of the fruits of modern labour on the other. And so in 1987 the World Commission on Environment and Development, the Brundtland Commission, called for new ways to look at the struggle between the environment and commerce. What emerged was the principle of sustainable development:

Sustainable development is development that meets the needs

of the present without compromising the ability of future generations to meet their own needs.

Sustainable development is said to focus on improving the quality of life for all of the earth's citizens without increasing the use of natural resources beyond the capacity of the environment to supply them indefinitely. The concept proposes that doing nothing is no longer an option since that too may bring unwelcome consequences This concept is encompassed in the European Union by the precautionary principle found in Article 174 of the EU Treaty. Thus it is necessary to find innovative ways fundamentally to change institutional structures and to influence individual behaviour. The IISD has said sustainable development 'is about taking action, changing policy and practice at all levels, from the individual to the international'.

However, sustainable development is not a new idea. Many cultures over the course of human history have recognised the need for harmony between the environment, society and economy. What is new is an articulation of these ideas in the context of a global industrial and informed society.

Progress on developing the concepts of sustainable development has been rapid since the 1980s. In 1992 leaders at the United Nations Conference on environment and Development (UNCED), the Earth Summit, built upon the framework of the Brundtland Commission to create agreements and conventions on critical issues such as climate change, desertification and deforestation. They also drafted a broad action strategy, Agenda 21, as the workplan for environment and development issues into the coming century. Throughout the rest of the 1990s, regional and sectoral sustainability plans were developed. A wide variety of groups – businesses, governments, international organisations such as the World Bank, – have adopted the concept and given it their own particular interpretations. These initiatives have increased understanding of what sustainable development means within a wide variety of contexts.

However, many businesses still find the term 'sustainable development' abstract, a concept with which it is difficult to connect. It may be useful therefore to consider this definition:

> To ensure a better quality of life for everyone, now and for generations to come (UK DETR definition).

This definition is perhaps even easier to visualise:

> The Earth is a spaceship hurtling through silent darkness, its inhabitants compelled forever to survive on what the spaceship carries.[4]

And by extension, that spaceship must deal with the waste produced from the activities of its inhabitants.

Sustainable development matters because the need for growth is as great as ever, especially in the developing world; and with the world's population forecast to increase from 6 billion to 10 billion over 50 years, there is overwhelming pressure to produce food cheaply and in the right places. Yet the environment is struggling to cope even with current levels of population and consumption.

THE EUROPEAN UNION

Present at UNCED and indeed taking a leading part in it was the European Union. Interested in the concepts of sustainable development, it considered the conclusion that sustainable development should be the governing rule behind environmental legislation and therefore that priority should be given among other matters to reuse and recycling, particularly with respect to waste. The EU deemed this to be of fundamental importance and so incorporated it as another of the cornerstone principles to which reference has already been made. Thus it appears in Article 174 of the amended Treaty and was a strategic part of the Fifth Action Programme on the environment with which the EU worked throughout the 1990s.

The EU sees sustainable development as a continuously evolving part of the environmental patchwork. For example, following a UNEP international round table on finance and the environment, late in 1998 it hosted Challenge for the Financial Sector, a workshop on sustainable development. There it was suggested that insurers, banks and other lending institutions could play a critical part in ensuring that industry put sustainable development at the heart of

[4] This idea was first propounded by Kenneth H. Boulding, Washington State University in 1965.

its business objectives, by rewarding those that did and penalising those that did not. This should perhaps be seen as part of the overall pattern of ensuring environmental compliance. It was also suggested that governments could lead industry by example and ensure compliance by legislation, if necessary.

While it is not difficult to support the principle that good accountants would be the first to advance: live on interest, preserve the capital (another definition of sustainable development), acceptable substitutes for our present way of life must be sought. Other less harmful means to provide what is needed must be found and we must measure our attempts at improvement, so we have tangible evidence to help us map the route. But how should sustainable development be measured? The Brundtland Commission called for the development of new ways to assess and measure progress, and much work has been and is being done to develop benchmarks and to establish those benchmarks for use internationally, nationally and at local and business level.

THE BELLAGIO PRINCIPLES

In 1996 an international group of environmental measurement practitioners and researchers met together in Bellagio, Italy. Their intention was to review what steps had been taken to produce environmental indicators and measurement tools and to provide an internationally recognised series of guidelines for the whole of the sustainable development assessment process, including the design and choice of indicators, their interpretation and communication of the results. It was intended that the indicators should be used as a complete set – no pick and mix for these academicians – and that they should be as valuable in the developed world as in the developing world. The principles were to be of use both in starting to measure progress towards sustainablility and as a yardstick for improving upon previous efforts. They are as useful for local communities as for governments, international organisations and private companies.

Overarching principles were sought that would provide a link between theory and practice. Such principles serve as practical guidelines for the whole of the assessment process. They deal with four aspects of assessing progress towards sustainable development:

from establishing the goal through to achievement. Principle 1 deals with the starting point of any assessment by establishing a vision of sustainable development and clear goals that provide a practical definition of that vision in terms that are meaningful for the decision-making unit in question. Principles 2 to 5 deal with the content of any assessment and the need to merge a sense of the overall system with a practical focus on current priority issues. Principles 6 to 8 deal with key issues of the process of assessment, while Principles 9 and 10 deal with the necessity for establishing a continuing capacity for assessment.

Briefly the principles may be summarised as follows:[5]

Guiding Vision and Goals
Assessment of progress toward sustainability should be guided by a clear vision of sustainable development and goals that define that vision.

Holistic Perspective
Assessment of progress toward sustainability should include review of the whole system being considered as well as its parts. Consider the well-being (including the state as well as the direction and rate of change of that state) of human, ecological, and economic sub-systems, their component parts, and the interaction between parts. Consider both positive and negative consequences of human activity, in a way that reflects the full costs and benefits for human and ecological systems, in monetary and non-monetary terms.

Essential Elements
Assessment of progress toward sustainability should consider equity and disparity within the current population and between current and future generations, dealing with such concerns as over-consumption and poverty, human rights, and access to services as appropriate. Consider the ecological conditions on which life depends.

---

[5] Our grateful thanks to IISD for allowing us to publish the principles in full. They may be found on the IISD website www.iisd.org and in Assessing Sustainable Development – The Principles in Practice, IISD, 1997.

Consider the success of economic development and other non-market activities that contribute to human/social well-being.

Adequate Scope

Assessment of progress toward sustainability should adopt a time horizon long enough to capture both human and ecosystem time scales thus responding to current short-term decision-making needs as well as those of future generations.

Define the space of study large enough to include not only local but also long-distance impacts on people and ecosystems. Build on historic and current conditions to anticipate future conditions.

Practical Focus

Assessment of progress toward sustainability should be based on an explicit set of categories or an organizing framework that links vision and goals to indicators and assessment criteria. A limited number of key issues for analysis. A limited number of indicators or indicator combinations to provide a clearer signal of progress.

Standardizing measurement wherever possible to permit comparison. Comparing indicator values to targets, reference values, ranges, thresholds, or direction of trends as appropriate.

Openness

Assessment of progress toward sustainability should make the methods and data that are used accessible to all. Make explicit all judgments, assumptions, and uncertainties in data and interpretations.

Effective Communication

Assessment of progress toward sustainability should be designed to address the needs of a specific audience and set of users. Draw from indicators and other tools that are stimulating and serve to engage decision-makers. From the outset, aim for simplicity in structure and use of clear and plain language.

21

Broad Participation

Assessment of progress toward sustainability should obtain broad representation of key grass-roots, social, professional, and technical groups to ensure recognition of diverse and changing values. Ensure decision-makers' participation thus securing a firm link to decision-making and resulting action.

Ongoing Assessment

Assessment of progress toward sustainability should encourage development of a capacity for repeated measurement to determine trends. Be iterative, adaptive, and responsive to change and uncertainty, because systems are complex and changing. Adjust goals, frameworks, and indicators as new insights are gained. Promote development of collective learning and feedback to decision-making.

Institutional Capacity

Continuity of assessing progress toward sustainability should be assured by clearly assigning responsibility and providing ongoing support in the decision-making process. Providing institutional capacity for data collection, maintenance, and documentation. Supporting development of local assessment capacity.

Following the Bellagio Principles came a welter of performance indicators at all sorts of levels. Particularly notable are the Environmental Performance Evaluation Guidelines issued by the European Committee for Standardisation as part of the ISO 14000 family of environmental management standards. Environmental Performance Evaluation (EPE) is a process of collection and assessment of data and information. It helps to provide an ongoing evaluation of performance and enables organisations to assess their environmental performance against a number of criteria, for example environmental policy, objectives and targets. EPE as a benchmarking tool will enable the company to benchmark against similar organisations to ensure that it is performing no worse (and hopefully better) than its competitors. Moreover, EPEs will help the company identify areas where improvement is needed as well as performance trends over time.

It is not difficult to see how this can feed back into the overall search for more sustainable business objectives which make up a critical part of sustainable development.

The UK government's approach to sustainable development throws yet a different light on this subject. In its new website published in 2001, www.sustainabledevelopment.gov.uk, the government in its Guiding Principles and Approaches says that their 'policies will also take account of ten principles and approaches which reflect key sustainable development themes'. Some are established legal principles. Others might better be described as 'approaches to decision making'. These principles are set out as follows:

- Putting people at the centre
- Taking a long-term perspective
- Taking account of costs and benefits
- Creating an open and supportive economic system
- Combating poverty and social exclusion;
- Respecting environmental limits;
- The precautionary principle
- Using scientific knowledge
- Transparency, information, participation and access to justice
- Making the polluter pay.

But principles, while laudable, do not really address what may be viewed as the ultimate challenge: Is industrial activity with its primary focus on profit and regulated by imperfect political organisations compatible with sustainable development? At first blush, the answer to this question would seem to be no. However, it may be argued that the Brundtland definition of sustainable development referred to earlier, views the environment as a means whereby people enjoy certain living standards, not something to be valued for its own sake. Developing this theme, profit-motivated business should require the most effective and efficient means to muster and use resources whether they be natural, financial or human. Thus, sustainable development principles are simply an arm of that requirement. This argument is, however, in the authors' view, a specious one. The reality is that it is difficult to reconcile sustainable development and business. For example, how should division between the needs of the current generation and future generations be apportioned? How should there be apportionment between those within the same generation? Human needs in different parts of the world differ greatly. It is only the first world that sets such great store by material wealth and the need for "things"; simpler societies have fewer material needs although the quality of life may be much higher. But it should not be forgotten that even within the same society there are different degrees of wealth and of needs. A proper analysis of Brundtland gives rise to some fundamental questions:

- Does the definition refer only to basic needs: food, shelter, etc.?
- Does it refer to quality of life and material objects?
- Does it refer to quality of the air, water, food, the land and landscape?
- Is it a combination of all of these?

In fact, could it not be said that sustainable development is a combination of all these issues and accordingly of social rather than environmental importance? These are not easy questions to answer, and indeed there may be no answers. What may be identified without too much difficulty is the impact that one action may have on another environmental aspect. For example, reduction of landfill capacity to meet EU targets may result in a greater need for incineration capacity. This in turn may impact on air quality. So, while on the one hand, the landscape is improved by the reduction in landfill sites, it may be sullied by the presence of large incinerators, and although the odour from landfill sites may be reduced, there may in its place be odour and emissions from the incineration process.

However, there will be circumstances where business is in a win-win position. For example, in relation to reduction and reuse of 'waste'. There is a discussion of waste issues on page 14, but from the standpoint of sustainable development, it should be recognised that there are also cost savings to be made. If new industrial techniques are introduced which minimise the waste created, this impacts on the amount of waste being disposed of at cost to business, reduces the dissipation of valuable resources and improves the financial bottom line. There will be other times when there must be a trade-off between the needs of sustainable development and the profitability of business. At these times there must be engagement between the business and its stakeholders, resulting perhaps in a partnership towards a shared vision of what sustainable development might imply.

Chapter 3 looks at the adverse effect on reputation of some environmental issues. Recent history shows that disquiet and disaster can play a prominent role in driving forward the environmental agenda. With the passage of time we become more fearful and less able to cope with the unknown. The consequences of some actions can be so unpredictable and so far outside our control as to render it difficult for us to deal with them. It is this unpredictability and uncontrollability that companies try to diminish, but in case after case, environmental disasters dramatically heightened by media reporting have triggered changes in public policy and company strategy. Notable examples are Shell and BP, where shareholder activism has impacted on the conduct of the business. Sometimes though, at any rate from a national perspective, the reverse is true.

There has been considerable public debate about the effects on the environment of carbon dioxide (CO_2) emissions, yet the Bush administration, apparently flying in the face of public pressure, has resolutely turned away from the Kyoto Protocol and left the rest of the world to make whatever arrangements for CO_2 reduction it deems appropriate. While some might call such action irresponsible, others, including President Bush, would claim that the US government is simply putting the needs of the American people first. This attitude is reducible to an individual company whose focus is solely on the financial bottom line and not the environment.

Employees too can impact on a company's view of sustainable development issues, for employees can permeate a company with attitudes and values which reflect more than the narrow view of profit above all. There are many examples of case studies evidencing the power of senior managers to change the thinking at board level, and many examples of such pioneering work failing because inadequate training in environmental issues was offered to the workforce. It is right that if environmental issues are to have a strong place in the culture of a company then change must be driven from the top, not by command and control but by consensus, training and demonstration of the benefits that such change can have on the environment. If this is done properly then business may move towards the ultimate goal of achieving sustainable development and the assumption of social responsibilities.

CONCLUSION

Many view stabilising climate change as the main environmental challenge facing mankind today. A short discussion on population growth has been included in this chapter as there is a causal link between it and the rate at which mankind is continuing to damage the environment. Success on these issues would make many other environmental issues more manageable, such as maintenance of water resources, forests and fish stocks. Although reducing the rate of population growth will undoubtedly present investment opportunities in health services and education in developing countries, it is primarily a behavioural change issue.

Returning to the environment issue, acceptance of the need to manage mankind's long-term impact on the environment is no longer the interest only of idealistic individuals and pressure groups; it is now a subject of intergovernmental policy and legislation. Detractors, particularly in the United States, cite the Kyoto Protocol on climate change as an example of where fundamental commitment to change is lacking. However, on the other side of the Atlantic, Europe has taken to the principles of climate change and driven through the next stage of the protocol, keeping countries other than the United States but including Japan committed to the principles, and introduced economic instruments to influence business behaviour. Other signs that the environment is moving to centre stage are evident from the Montreal Protocol on the use of ozone-depleting substances and the Basel Convention on the Transboundary Shipment of Waste.

Climate change and the other environmental issues discussed in this chapter could be described as the next frontier so far as business opportunities are concerned. Two hundred years ago the Industrial Revolution became a driver for change and created endless opportunities for business. The IT revolution of the 1990s and beyond offered another challenge to the old order and opportunities for the new. Now it seems that the environment will force an even more fundamental change in the conditions of business. Companies that ignore this message will do so at their peril. Reducing mankind's impact on the atmosphere will require a complete overhaul of the energy economy both to reduce reliance on fossil fuels and to drive down harmful emissions. Belief in one or other of the arguments advanced by the IPCC or the solar activists is immaterial. The fact is that many countries have translated climate change concerns into legal action and expect to see public health as well as environmental benefits. The environmental genie may not yet be fully out of the bottle but it is unlikely to be put back.

Importantly, the climate change debate has prompted a review of how mankind's energy needs should be met in the future. Not surprisingly, given mankind's historical dependence on fossil fuels and the vast investment made in supporting infrastructure, little mainstream business attention has been paid to technological developments which would enable a move away from reliance on fossil fuels. Today, however, options such as solar power, wind and tidal energy, and microgeneration are emerging not only as viable alternatives but as essential options if the world is to meet its long-term energy needs. Similarly, the increasing concern over global water supplies has focused attention on the need to conserve supplies by reducing pollution and by increasing the efficiency of irrigation and other agricultural, industrial and domestic uses of fresh water. But business will also have to look at other areas where efficiency is required if the earth's limited resources are not to be depleted. Economic logic, intelligent use of technology and innovative design must be bought to bear to wring more benefit from each measure of energy or material consumed. Economies must move from dependence on the acquisition of goods and their use and disposal to a zero-waste culture.

The market is coming and smart businesses will be preparing to take advantage of it. One way they can do so is to watch very carefully the emerging debate on sustainable development.

CHAPTER 2

The Rapid Development of Environmental Law

INTRODUCTION

Environmental law, like the environment itself, is not simple. Both are a patchwork of pieces that touch and often overlap. Although a relatively new subject, environmental law has developed rapidly and quickly become a specialist topic. Its complexity is attributable to the significance of the legal and policy developments that occur at a national level and on a global basis. On any environmental issue it may be necessary to consider a wide variety of sources of law and regulation. These may include treaties, conventions, protocols, EU regulations and directives and domestic law. A further complication is that environmental law is, as will be seen, still evolving and while principles may have been established, much detail remains to be painted in before the picture is complete. Thus it often happens that advice must be given and action taken on the basis not only of the law as it is, but as it is anticipated it will be in the short to medium term.

This force of environmental law has major commercial implications. The decisions made today must in some sense reflect the policies just in being and likely to be implemented in the future – for if they do not, business runs a real risk of making expensive mistakes. Assistance in trying to predict the future course of environmental legislation can be gained from looking outside domestic law to the two perhaps greatest influences on the scope and direction of policy and regulation, namely the United States and Europe. And so this chapter investigates the way in which environmental law has developed in the United States and in the EU, compares the two and offers a view of the core law topics of air, water and land.

Traditionally environmental law was divided into topics but over the last two decades there has been a blurring of the issues and other more universal matters have come to the fore, such as sustainable development, global warming, waste management issues and genetically modified organisms. Sometimes these matters cut across the traditional areas, but the first two have their place in this discussion as drivers for improved environmental performance (Chapter 1), and waste management issues are considered elsewhere in this book.

Although many may understand the legislative processes which result in the making of law, many others will not and might therefore find it helpful to begin with the following brief and simplified description.

HOW US LAW IS MADE

Article I, Section 1, of the US Constitution, establishes the legislative function by creating Congress in these words: 'All Legislative Powers herein granted shall be vested in a Congress of the United States, which shall consist of a Senate and House of Representatives.'

The majority of laws originate in the House of Representatives, although both the Senate and the House of Representatives have more or less equal legislative functions and powers. The principal difference is that the Constitution provides that only the House of Representatives may originate revenue bills. Similarly, it should be noted that in the UK only the House of Commons (the elected chamber of the UK Parliament) can initiate finance bills.

The chief function of Congress is the making of laws, although in addition, the Senate has the function of advising and consenting to treaties and to certain nominations made by the President. However, under the 25th Amendment to the Constitution, both Houses confirm the President's nomination for vice-president when there is a vacancy in that office.

Sources of ideas for legislation are unlimited and proposed drafts of bills originate in many diverse quarters. First among these is, as might be expected, the proposal submitted by a member or delegate. This may be on the sole initiative of the member, or because he has been petitioned by his constituents to put forward a draft bill. The right of citizens to petition their representative is guaranteed by the First Amendment to the Constitution. The member may ask the Legislative Counsel of the House or the Senate for drafting assistance to ensure that the bill is framed in suitable language and appropriate form. (In the UK the parliamentary draftsman performs the same task for government.)

Once a bill is proposed it is referred, by the Speaker, to the appropriate committee or committees as required by the rules of the House. The committees undertake detailed scrutiny of a proposed measure and provide the forum where the public is given its opportunity to be heard. Membership on the various committees is divided between the two major political parties One of the first actions taken by a committee is to seek the input of the relevant departments and agencies; for a bill with environmental content, the principal agency is the Environmental Protection Agency (EPA). Frequently, the bill is also submitted to the General Accounting Office with a request for an official report of views on the necessity or desirability of enacting it into law. These reports are not binding on the committee If the bill is of sufficient importance, the committee may set a date for public hearings.

If the committee votes to report the bill to the House, the committee staff writes a report, describing its purpose and scope and the reasons for its recommended approval. After general debate, the second reading of the bill begins. The second reading is a section-by-section reading during which time germane amendments may be offered to a section when it is read. At the end of debate on the second reading, the Speaker then puts the question, 'Shall the bill be engrossed and read a third time?' If the answer is 'yes', the bill is read a third time by title only and voted on for passage. It then goes to the other house, where it receives three readings, in the same way as just described.

If both houses of Congress approve a bill and all issues relating to amendments proposed by the second house are resolved by the first, the bill is enrolled and checked for accuracy. It is then presented to the President, who has the option to either approve it or veto it. Notice of the signing of a bill by the President is sent by message to the house in which it originated, and that house informs the other. The action is also noted in the Congressional Record. At the point it is approved by the President it ceases to be called a bill; it is now called an act and is law.

Contrast this with the position in England. The UK Parliament is divided into two chambers, the House of Commons, the elected chamber, and the House of Lords, currently being reformed to provide a membership not comprising solely hereditary peers and appointed representatives. As in the American system, a bill may originate in either House, promoted by the government or by a private member. A private member's bill has little chance of success unless taken over by government. This is because of the pressure on parliamentary time. A bill, wherever it originates, receives a first presentation at which simply the name of the bill is read out (the First Reading). This signifies authority for the bill to be printed Once the bill is printed it proceeds to its first substantive stage – the Second Reading. This gives opportunity for a wide ranging debate, usually of the whole House, on the principle of the bill. There then follows the committee stage which involves clause by clause consideration of the measure. The fourth stage, the report stage, is a detailed review of the bill as amended in committee. The fifth stage is known as the Third Reading and enables the House to take an overview of the bill. If passed it proceeds to the other chamber. There a broadly similar procedure is followed. As in Congress, committees are drawn from the members, weighted according to the political make-up of the parliament. For some bills the whole House forms the committee for the committee stage. In England a bill becomes an act once the Queen has signified her assent to it.

Once an act is passed, the practice in England and in the United States is somewhat different. In England the act immediately becomes law, although it may enter into force at a later date. The act may require detailed regulations to implement it. If it does then they are drafted by the appropriate government department. Often an act allows for regulations to be made on the negative basis. If so, then although they are tabled in Parliament, they receive no scrutiny and become law on the date stated on them.

However, it is possible, although rare, for such regulations to be nullified if either house passes a motion calling for their annulment. Less common than the negative procedure, is the affirmative procedure which requires the regulation to be laid before the House (Commons or Lords) for approval. It must then be approved by the other house. Most regulations dealt with under the affirmative procedure are considered by a standing committee prior to being laid before the House. Both acts and regulations are published by the Stationery Office.

In the United States, the House of Representatives standardises the text of the law and publishes it in the United States Code. The US Code is the official record of all federal laws. However, an act itself is often simply a framework setting out the principles of the law. The detail is then supplied by regulations. In order to make the laws work on a day-to-day level, Congress authorises certain government agencies, including the EPA to create regulations.

Regulations set specific rules about what may and may not be done in particular circumstances. For example, a regulation issued by EPA to implement the Clean Air Act might state what levels of a pollutant, such as sulphur dioxide, are safe. The regulations impose limits for emissions to the air, and what the penalty will be if they exceed the limits. English regulations are unlikely to contain such a level of detail, such matters are left to the Environment Agency to decide.

Before a US regulation can become law, the proposal for the regulation is listed in the Federal Register so that members of the public can consider it and send their comments to the government agency proposing it. The agency considers all the comments, revises the regulation if appropriate, and issues the document in its final form. At each stage in the process, the government agency must publish a notice in the Federal Register. These notices include the original proposal, requests for public comment, notices about meetings where the proposal will be discussed (open to the public), and the text of the final regulation. Twice a year, each government agency with the power to make regulations publishes a report describing all the regulations it is working on or has recently finished. These are published in the Federal Register. Once a regulation is completed and has been printed in the Federal Register as a final regulation, it is codified by being published in the Code of Federal Regulations (CFR). The CFR is the official record of all regulations created by the federal government. Almost all environmental regulations appear in Title 40. The CFR is revised yearly, Title 40 is revised every July 1.[1]

THE EU LEGISLATIVE SYSTEM

Before turning to the nature and extent of US environmental regulation, it is perhaps useful to compare the US legislative process with that of the EU. At first blush, there may appear to be some similarities between the US with its states and state assemblies, and the EU with its member countries and national parliaments. But the comparison is not fruitful since the EU member countries retain their sovereign rights and the EU, despite its title, is not a union of states but a much less constrained framework of nations.

If the workings of Congress appear complicated, the complications are as nothing compared with the complexities in the legislative and regulatory systems of the EU. And while most parliamentary systems are subjected only to the occasional upheaval – for example that being undergone in the UK to provide devolved powers for Scotland and a Welsh Assembly – that of the EU has altered rapidly over the years to meet the complaints of lack of transparency and lack of accountability of elected members. Plainly a full account of the EU institutions is not appropriate here and what follows is a brief and simplified description of law and policy-making in the EU.

There are five institutions engaged in running the European Union: the European Parliament (elected by the citizens of the member states), the European Council (representing the governments of the member states), the European Commission (the executive and the body having the right to initiate legislation), the Court of Justice (ensuring compliance with the law), and the Court of Auditors (responsible for auditing the accounts). These institutions are supported by other bodies, such as the Economic and Social Committee. Of the five primary institutions of the EU, the Commission is still the most important. Until the Maastricht and Amsterdam Treaties it

[1] With thanks to the Thomas Library of Congress from which most of the US material was drawn.

was seen, with some justification, as an all-powerful body control-ling the EU without any accountability. However, these treaties have given the Commission more democratic legitimacy by giving the European Parliament some control over the commission's functions.

The President of the Commission is chosen by EU heads of state or government meeting in the European Council. This choice has to be approved by the European Parliament. The other 19 members of the Commission are nominated by the governments of the 15 member states in agreement with the new commission president. The Presi-dent and the other members-designate are subject to a collective vote of approval by the European Parliament.

The system of parliamentary vetting of the President and the other Commissioners, instituted by the Treaty on European Union and reinforced by the Amsterdam Treaty, does much to allay criticism that the Commission is an unelected body without democratic legiti-macy. It gives the European Parliament a full voice in the choice or appointment of the President and the other Commissioners. Previously, its only power in this context (which it retains) was to force the resignation of the whole Commission through a vote of censure. It has never used this option. (although it came close to doing so in 1999, thus resulting in the resignation of the President at the time and all his Commissioners).

Two Commissioners come from each of Germany, Spain, France, Italy and the UK (the countries with the greater populations) and one from each of Belgium, Denmark, Greece, Ireland, Luxembourg, the Netherlands, Austria, Portugal, Finland and Sweden.

As the European Union has developed over the years, so the Commission has acquired new responsibilities. Remember that the beginnings of the EU are to be found in the European Coal and Steel Community, which came into being in 1951 to pool together the most essential materials required by industry, coal and steel. It developed from those humble beginnings to the European Economic Community with just 6 members, through to the European Union of 15 countries with more countries waiting to gain accession. The accession countries are Bulgaria, Cyprus, Czech Republic, Estonia, Hungary, Latvia, Lithuania, Malta, Poland, Romania, Slovak Repub-lic, Slovenia and Turkey. The Single European Act of 1986, incor-porating the first significant update of the founding treaties, the

Treaty on European Union and the Amsterdam Treaty all confirm and expand the scope of the Union.

The Commission initiates EU policy and represents the general interest of the EU. It fulfils three main functions; one of them is the making of proposals for all new legislation. It does so on the basis of what it considers best for the EU and its citizens in general rather than on behalf of sectoral interests or individual countries. Before it issues an item of draft legislation, the Commission carries out extensive preliminary soundings and discussions with representatives of governments, industry, the trade unions, special interest groups and, where necessary, technical experts. It tries to take account of these often competing interests when it prepares its proposals.

Once a Commission proposal has been submitted to the Council of Ministers and the European Parliament, the three institutions work together to produce a satisfactory result. In agreement with the Commission, the Council can amend a proposal using the qualified majority voting majority rule, but if the Commission does not agree, the change requires unanimity. The European Parliament shares the power of codecision with the European Council in most areas and has to be consulted in others. This puts the European Parliament and the European Council on an equal footing and leads to the adoption of joint European Council and European Parliament acts. Through the codecision procedure, many more parliamentary amendments find their way into EU laws and no text can now be adopted without the formal agreement of the European Parliament and the European Council. Environmental matters are dealt with using the codecision principle. The procedure was used, for example, by the European Parliament to secure much stricter rules on fuel quality and motor oil from the year 2000, in order to achieve drastic cuts in atmospheric pollution.

The codecision procedure has three stages: first reading, second reading and conciliation. The procedure can be concluded after each stage, if the two branches of legislative authority have reached an agreement. Once the conciliation process is completed, the Commission proposal becomes law. EU law is enacted chiefly as regulations or directives. Regulations have immediate binding effect on all the national states, that is they are enforceable in the national states without the need for further domestic legislation. Directives always contain a date by which they must take effect in the national state but cannot do so until transposed into national law. All legislation must be published in the official journal of the European Union and until published it has no binding force.

THE DEVELOPMENT OF ENVIRONMENTAL LAW

It is often said that the key driver for environmental improvement is legislation. This statement, however, gives rise to a fundamental question, Without environmental legislation would there be any drive towards environmental improvement? The probable answer is that legislation is one of several drivers but that as breach of environmental regulation in most countries falls to be dealt with under the criminal law system (breach of which can lead to fines or imprisonment or both) the need at the very least, to meet existing environmental regulation, is great.[2] Plainly in this book there is neither a need for, nor an interest in, the detail of environmental law but the core topics referred to earlier are of interest to demonstrate how the same problems can give rise to different or indeed the same solutions and how the relevant legislation does in fact drive business towards a more environmentally acceptable approach to manufacture, distribution and sale of product.

In the United States perhaps modern environmental law can be said to commence with the National Environmental Policy Act 1969 (NEPA). The Act was promulgated for the purposes of

> declaring a national policy to encourage productive and enjoy-
> able harmony between man and his environment; to promote
> efforts to prevent or eliminate damage to the environment and
> biosphere and stimulate the health and welfare of man; to
> enrich the understanding of the ecological systems and natural
> resources important to the Nation; and to establish a Council on
> Environmental Quality. (NEPA website)

In the European Union development was rather different. The European Economic Community was founded by the Treaty of

---

[2] In many countries legislation is extended so that not only can the business be fined but the responsible director or manager can face a prison sentence.

Rome in 1957. From modest beginnings it has grown to the European Union of 15 countries seen today (with a number of accession countries presently waiting for admission). The Treaty contained nothing relating to the environment or its protection, which perhaps is unsurprising, given that the environment in the decade following the Second World War was not on any agenda. It was not until 1973, with the first Environmental Action Programme, that there was a recognition of environmental issues and not until 1986, with the implementation of the Single European Act followed some years later by the Maastricht Treaty and then the Amsterdam Treaty, that specific treaty authority was offered for environmental legislation.

While it would be wrong to reduce European environmental legislation to a series of principles, nevertheless at the heart of the complex web of legislation lie a number of fundamental policies which influence all legislation. These 'cornerstone' principles are to be found in the Treaty of Amsterdam (which incorporates the previous treaties and renumbers them). Article 2 of the Treaty contains the requirements for sustainable development and improvement of the quality of the environment and human health. Article 6 contains the requirement to integrate the environment into EU policies. Articles 174–176 are the remainder of the cornerstone principles, which may be summarised thus: polluter pays, prevention, precaution, subsidiarity, proximity and proportionality. Their thread is woven throughout environmental and increasingly other EU legislation. It is sufficient to describe briefly the purpose of each of these policies and if they are kept firmly in mind then business, in Europe at least, will understand whereabouts environmental legislation is driving it.

Polluter pays

The literal meaning is easy to understand: he who pollutes must pay for the consequences of his actions. However, there is an extended version which suggests that everyone from the producer of the raw material, through the manufacturer of the product to its distribution, use and disposal, may bear a share of responsibility for pollution caused, and this extended definition is reflected in the Civil Liability White Paper currently being considered throughout the EU.

Prevention

This principle is plain: environmental damage should be prevented. Again it is capable of an extended definition, not merely that regulators should take steps early to prevent damage being caused but that such actions should be taken irrespective of the strength of proof that they are required.

Precaution

It is not perhaps as easy to understand the precautionary principle, since there is an underlying moral connotation to use good husbandry in the treatment of natural resources. In England in 2000 the precautionary principle was much in evidence when protestors sought to prevent the growing of genetically modified seeds so that there would be no possibility of harm to the environment through the inadvertant spread of seeds.

Subsidiarity

This principle is designed to ensure that EU environmental law represents the minimum acceptable standards, thus leaving member states free to regulate more strictly if so inclined.

Proximity

The intention governing this principle is that environmental damage should be remedied at its source. It relates particularly to waste so that waste must be disposed of as close as possible to the point of generation.

Proportionality

This final principle provides that the terms and extent of any obligations imposed by the EU must be reasonably related to the objectives sought. It can be further extended so that the cost of compliance must be proportionate to the benefit to the environment.

Time for some detail

With these principles in mind it is now time to look at the detail of some environmental statutes. It is difficult to make a selection by importance between pollution of the land, the water and the atmosphere. There can be no doubt, however, that nothing causes greater concern in a local population (whether in Europe or the United States or indeed anywhere else in the world) than the sight of an industrial chimney issuing forth a plume of black smoke, whether or not accompanied by chemical releases or showers of sparks.

US LAW ON THE ATMOSPHERE

In the United States the Clean Air Act 1970 set out to address the fundamental problems caused by unregulated emissions to atmosphere by regulating discharges from area, stationary and mobile sources. It is perhaps worth pointing out that probably the greatest source of air pollution in fact comes from mobile sources, e.g. vehicle emissions. The EPA was authorised to set up National Ambient Air Quality Standards (NAAQS) to protect public health and the environment. Coupled with this was a requirement upon each state to develop and implement plans to comply with the NAAQS.[3] The Act has been amended on several occasions. Like its predecessors, this Act is a federal act, with the states implementing the detail of the legislation. The EPA is charged with setting limits on how much of any pollutant can be released into the air. States that wish to do so may implement stricter regulations, but no state can apply regulations that are less stringent. It is said by the EPA that

> the law recognises that it makes sense for states to take the lead in carrying out the Clean Air Act 1990 because pollution control problems often require special understanding of local industry, housing patterns etc. (Office of Air Quality Planning and Standards, *Plain English Guide to the Clean Air Act 1990*)

While in limited circumstances there may need to be a 'special understanding' of local industries, it must follow that polluting

---

[3] This method of legislation is very similar to that adopted by the EU, where with its directives it requires member states to develop and implement its own detailed legislation. With air quality the nature of the legislation, too, is similar.

industries will seek out states with the minimum standards and avoid, where possible, those that have implemented regulation above the minimum standards set federally.

It was not until the 1990 Act that there was introduced a system for authorising larger industrial plants that release pollutants into the atmosphere. These permits are issued at state level or where the state fails to implement the Clean Air Act satisfactorily, by the EPA. The permit indicates what pollutants are being emitted, the allowable quantities of such emissions, pollution reduction policy and monitoring.

The Act also contains market approaches for reducing air pollution; for example, the acid rain clean-up programme offers businesses choices as to how to meet pollution reduction targets and provides for pollution allowances that may be traded, i.e. bought and sold. Moreover, the act also introduces a credit system so that more efficient producers exceeding their targets can obtain credits that may be used if on another occasion they fail to meet the standard set. Economic instruments are becoming increasingly important as a means of rewarding business for environmental improvement and punishing business for its polluting excesses.

To understand the scale of the problem, it helps to know that the EPA suggests that industrial operations emit nearly 100 million US tons of pollutants into the air each year. This includes sulphur dioxide, carbon monoxide, benzene, mercury and dioxins. As already noted, the Act requires all states to develop and implement an operating permit programme that meets federal minimum requirements. Most of the significant air pollution sources throughout the United States must obtain a permit from the state, tribal or local permitting authority. Each state and local government can tailor its permit programme to its individual needs, so long as it meets federal requirements. All major polluting installations must obtain an operating permit. Whether an installation is 'major' depends on the type and amount of its air pollutants and in some respects the background air quality will impact on the amount of substances which may be emitted. Major sources are generally regarded as those that emit more than 100 US tons or more per annum of a regulated air pollutant. In addition to the pollutants noted above, the regulations also cover particulates and volatile organic compounds. As alluded to earlier, if the background air quality is poor, facilities which do not emit such high amounts of pollutants but perhaps only 25 US tons per annum or even less, may nevertheless be regarded as major for the purpose of the regulations. Moreover, sources of toxic air pollutants, that is any source that emits more than 10 US tons per annum of an individual toxic pollutant, or more than 25 US tons per annum of any combination of toxic air pollutants, may be covered by the programme.

The air pollution permitting programme follows the system laid down in the Clean Water Act (page 45). The regulations provide for submission of biannual emissions reports and annual certification of compliance status. Permits must be renewed, generally every five years and fees are charged by the licensing authorities, usually on the basis of the amount of air pollutants emitted. The public, of course, have the right to be consulted and to make representations, both when a new permit application is made and when an existing permit falls to be revised or renewed. The EPA has retained overall control and supervision of the permit programme and may raise objection to a permit that does not comply with the programme plan. It is interesting to compare this system with that operating in England and to note that the US system contains a commitment to continuous improvement as required by many environmental management systems.

EU AIR POLLUTION REGULATION

Although historically there were some isolated pieces of air pollution legislation at EU level, many of the member states were more advanced than the EU in recognising and providing for the effects of air pollution. This changed in 1996, however, when the Air Quality Framework Directive (Council Directive 96/62/EC) was adopted. This Directive sets the basic principles of a common strategy: defining, establishing and assessing the objectives for ambient air quality in the EU using common methods and criteria; producing adequate information on ambient air quality and ensuring its availability to the public. The Directive also proposes maintenance of ambient air quality where it is good and seeks methods to improve it where it is not.

The Directive requires member states:

- To designate zones and agglomerations covering the whole territory and then to draw up lists of those zones or agglomerations where the level of pollutants is higher than prescribed and lists of those areas where the level is lower than prescribed.
- To undertake a series of representative measures surveys or assessments to obtain preliminary data on the levels of pollutants in the air.
- To draw up action plans to ensure that limits are not exceeded in areas where there is a risk that they may be and where the limits are exceeded to draw up plans to ensure compliance within a specified period of time.
- Where levels are lower than prescribed, to ensure that those lower levels are maintained consistent with the principles of sustainable development.

As in the United States, the largest single source of air pollution is not from industrial installations but from vehicles, and vehicle emission levels led to a consideration of the implications of the Kyoto Protocol both for industry and for individuals (Chapter 1). It is clear that a radical rethink will be required encompassing the way in which raw materials are delivered to a plant, the way they are handled within the plant (still often by forklift truck driven by petrol or diesel) and the way finished products are delivered to the wholesaler, retailer and then the ultimate consumer. All of these stages presently rely heavily on road transport. However, this rethink must extend beyond the role of heavy vehicles to the ways employees travel to their place of business, the method of transport that is used between branches of the same business and the methods of transport used by representatives, whether buying or selling product. Finally there must be detailed consideration of the habits of the travelling consumer.

Where the United States Clean Air Act and the EU Directive diverge is in the controls exercised over industrial plant. While the US law contains provision relating to industry, the directive does not. The principal EU regulation relating to industrial plants is Directive 96/61/EC on integrated pollution prevention and control. The EU system is designed to provide a single regulatory framework to cover all pollution emissions from industrial processes, that is from land, air and water. To the extent that this also encompasses the areas already covered by Directive 76/464/EC on water pollution by dangerous substances and Directive 84/360/EC on air pollution from industrial plants, there is some duplication. But the stated intention of the Directive is to modify and supplement existing EU legislation concerning the prevention and control of pollution from industrial plants in order to achieve an integrated approach to the reduction and prevention of pollution. The Directive already applies to permits for plants built since October 1999 and all other relevant installations are being phased in over a period up to 2007.

All installations covered by the Directive (and these are essentially the most polluting industries) are required to obtain a permit without which they may not operate. Permits are usually issued by the environment agency in the member state (the licensing authority). The permit is based on the concept of best available technique (BAT). A definition of BAT is to be found in the Directive and in the English transposing regulations. However, it is clear that the exact meaning of the expression in relation to any particular piece of plant or equipment may give rise to considerable argument. In order to minimise the scope of such argument, a European IPPC Bureau (established by the European Commission) provides assistance to licensing authorities. The Bureau is divided into about 30 sectors following the industrial groupings contained in the Directive. It issues BAT reference documents (BREFs) detailing what amounts to BAT for the particular industry sector. BREFs are non-binding guidance documents that will serve as benchmarks for national pollution control authorities when they set permit conditions for industrial installations under IPPC. Notwithstanding the contents of any particular BREF, of course, the licensing authority is still able to make the final decision concerning what amounts to BAT in any specific circumstance. It is said that IPPC takes a more holistic approach to permitting. This is because it requires the operator not only to look for ways to reduce polluting emissions to land, water and air but because as a general condition it requires consideration to be given to the use of low-waste technology, less hazardous substances, and the consumption and nature of raw materials.

There is no similar system in the United States, where three separate pieces of legislation govern air, water and land, hence three separate authorisations to pollute are required. However, there are certain similarities between the US air pollution control system and the English Integrated Pollution Control (IPC) and Local Authority Air Pollution Control (LAAPC) regimes. Both detail the pollutants and provide for emission levels, both provide that plant cannot operate without the necessary permit. In England IPC authorisations are handled by the Environment Agency whereas LAAPC authorisations are handled by local authorities; IPC authorisations cover all polluting media, LAAPC covers only air pollution. All authorisations are subject to review by the issuing authority every four years (not five as in the United States) and in England there are significant opportunities for public consultation and for the public to make its voice heard. Both IPC and LAAPC will be phased out of English regulation as the Pollution Prevention and Control regime begins to take effect. The regulations came into force in England in October 2000 and take effect over various industry sectors over a period ending in 2007 as required by the EU Directive.

WATER REGULATION IN THE US

The principle enabling legislation is the Federal Water Pollution Control Act 1972 as amended by the Clean Water Act 1977 (CWA). The purpose of the legislation is to make it unlawful for any person to discharge any pollutant from a point source into a water of the United States unless permitted to do so. The Act gives authority to the EPA to set effluent standards on an industry basis and water quality standards for all contaminants to surface waters. The CWA was amended again in 1987, the amendments in both cases directed, among other things, towards toxic pollutants.

The National Pollutant Discharge Elimination System (NPDES) permit contains discharge limits, as well as monitoring and reporting requirements. The term 'pollutant' is defined widely in the CWA; broadly it includes any type of industrial, municipal and agricultural waste discharged into water. 'Point source' has a wide definition and encompasses 'any discernible confined and discrete conveyance such as a pipe, ditch, channel, tunnel, conduit, discrete fissure or container' (Office of Wastewater Management, EPA). It also includes,

45

vessels or other floating craft and concentrated animal feeding operations. Lastly 'a water of the United States' is defined as navigable waters, interstate waters, the oceans out to 200 miles, and intrastate waters which are used by interstate travellers for recreation or other purposes as a source of fish and shellfish sold in interstate commerce or for industrial purposes by industrial organisations engaged in interstate commerce.

An NPDES permit is required if the discharge is a pollutant, from a point source into a United States water. If it is not, for example because discharge is to a municipal sanitary sewer, then no NPDES permit is required although it may require local consent. If, however, the discharge is to a municipal storm sewer then an NPDES permit may be required. This is because there are different standards of water treatment applied to water in a storm sewer and water in a sanitary sewer. If a permit is necessary, it will be obtained from the state if authorised by the EPA to issue permits; and if not, by the EPA itself.

Once obtained, the NPDES permit is in force for five years. It can be renewed on application by the holder and it can be varied if circumstances require it. A permit can also be administratively renewed at the end of the five-year period if the holder applies more than 180 days before the expiry date. and the licensing authority agrees to an extension. There is provision for the public notification and participation in the permitting process.

EU WATER LAW

There is a plethora of legislation covering water issues; indeed water pollution problems represented the first environmental area in which the EU took legislative action as long ago as 1973. The last thirty years have seen almost forty directives, decisions and other measures designed to protect and enhance the water environment. Water legislation until 2000 fell into two distinct groups, one part aimed at imposing water quality standards, the other at minimising water pollution. It is with the pollution category that we are concerned here. The 1976 Directive 76/464/EC establishes the framework under which the discharge of listed substances into inland surface waters, territorial waters and internal coastal waters are controlled throughout the EU. Member states are given the option of meeting the standards by either imposing limit values which must not be exceeded in a discharge containing the substance (this is the system adopted under the United States CWA) or by setting environmental quality objectives so that the concentration of the substance in the receiving water does not exceed the relevant standard. (This is the system adopted by the UK.)

The directive has been enhanced from time to time by further legislation but it was not until 2000 that a new Water Framework Directive (WFD) was adopted, bringing together the two groups of regulation referred to earlier. This wide-reaching piece of legislation (Directive 2000/60/EC) has several main elements. It protects all waters including all surface and ground waters. This takes account for the first time of the integral connection between water quality and quantity. The WFD contains ambitious quality objectives and all waters must achieve 'good status' by 2015. If there are to be derogations, these will be linked to clear conditions. For groundwater 'good status' means achieving a sustainable balance between abstractions and natural recharge as well as implementing a proper ecological dimension. There are further emission controls and water quality objectives, and particularly hazardous substances are to be phased out entirely. The WFD aims to change the pattern of water use – following the polluter pays principle – and the principle of recovery of costs of water services, with a view to achieving the integration of the full cost of water use into the price paid. The intention being that this will lead to a more rational and sustainable use. Lastly the WFD ensures that all measures on water policy work together by requiring that actions are coordinated for each river basin. For this to work, each river basin must (and will) have a river basin management plan.

Remember that the IPPC Directive impacts on water legislation. Industry does not have to obtain separate permits for PPC and for water issues. In England, at any rate, one PPC permit will be issued which covers all polluting emissions over all environmental media. Of course, in the EU if the installation is not subject to the IPPC Directive then the business will need to make application to the licensing authority for a permit to discharge to water, and there may be a discharge to atmosphere which also requires to be permitted.

CONTAMINATED LAND: THE US PERSPECTIVE

From a business viewpoint one of the most important legislative drivers is contaminated land regulation. While the likelihood of facing a prison term by reason of a breach of the regulations is remote, the financial aspects may be considerable and adverse in the extreme. The law has developed in the United States and in Europe in different ways. In the United States the linchpin for the investigation and clean-up of sites onto which hazardous substances have been released is the Comprehensive Environmental Response, Compensation, and Liability Act 1980 (CERCLA). This Act introduced the Hazardous Substance Superfund, a tax on the petroleum and chemical industries providing broad authority to federal agencies to respond directly to actual or threatened releases of hazardous substances that might cause harm to human health or the environment. The Act was amended in 1986 by the Superfund Amendments and Reauthorisation Act (SARA). Superfund is theoretically available to finance the cleaning up of hazardous waste sites. Over five years $1.6 billion was collected. However, it is a sad fact that the overwhelming proportion of the funds collected went not to contaminated land clean-up but to pay lawyers' bills in fighting the obligations imposed by the legislation.

CERCLA has three main aspects:

- A comprehensive federal state mechanism for a rapid response to releases or threatened releases of hazardous substances into the environment at facilities where the owner or operator is unwilling or unable to do this.
- A federal trust fund financed in the main by private industry to pay the cost of response action by federal or state agencies or private volunteers.
- A federal cause of action for recovery of costs incurred for responses to hazardous substances releases from four categories of person – current owners and operators at the time of disposal, processors of the hazardous substances, and transporters who selected the facility.

It is this last aspect of CERCLA that has given rise to the multiplicity of claims and resulted in the Superfund being used to fund litigation rather than clean-up of contaminated sites. The EPA has an extensive armoury of enforcement options under CERCLA. These include the ability to require or compel responsible parties to take action; action to enforce a previously made order to clean up and for costs recovery (including the costs if EPA undertakes the clean-up itself); damages and federal liens.

SARA stressed the importance of permanent remedies and innovative treatment technologies in cleaning hazardous waste sites, required the EPA to revise the Hazard Ranking System, extended the focus on human health problems and increased the size of the trust fund to $8.5 billion.

EU CONTAMINATED LAND REGULATION

There is no adopted legislation for regulation and remediation of contaminated land sites in the EU, and absent any EU policy, a common approach for reporting on contaminated sites is to be developed by the European Environment Agency across Western Europe on a voluntary basis. A pilot scheme collating data from regions in ten European states is to be published in 2001. There is, however, some water and waste management legislation that impacts on contaminated land, and some EU countries have developed their individual contaminated land regimes. It is worth giving a brief description of the English system as it may indicate the possible direction of EU policy.

In England the fear of inherited liability, particularly within the financial community, is a specific force driving the need to consider and understand contaminated land issues – it is indeed one of the principal drivers for this book since it is estimated that land comprises over 30% of the asset base of UK manufacturing companies and 74% of all lendings are secured on land-based assets. Interest in this area surfaced after CERCLA was implemented in the United States but it took almost 20 years before England followed with an enforceable contaminated land regime. The first attempt at regulation in this field came with the Environmental Protection Act 1990, which envisaged the creation of contaminated land registers. However, the legislation was never implemented and it was replaced by a different regime in the Environment Act 1995. Even then it took five years for the implementing regulations to be framed and passed into law, and it was only in April 2000 that the regulations became part of English environmental law.

Contaminated land is defined as 'land which appears to the enforcing authority[4] to be in such a condition by reason of substances in, on or under it that significant harm is being caused or there is a significant possibility of such harm being caused or pollution of controlled waters is being or is likely to be caused harm is defined as harm to the health of living organisms or harm to the ecological systems of which they form part and in the case of man, includes his property'. There is, in addition, statutory remedy available in respect of controlled waters under the Water Resources Act 1991. 'Substance' is defined as any natural or artificial substance whether in solid, liquid vaporous or gaseous form. Contrast this with the United States, where the accent is not on the definition of contaminated land but on the release of hazardous substances onto the land. The substances are designated under CERCLA (unlike in England where any substance that contaminates may give rise to a claim for clean-up).

In England the accountable party (known in the Act as the 'appropriate person' is any person who 'caused or knowingly permitted any of the relevant substances to be in, on or under the land', or failing identification of such person, the owner or occupier for the time being of the land. Whether land will be regarded as contaminated for the purposes of the Contaminated Land Regulations 2000 depends on whether it remains suitable for use. If it does and there is no escape of the contaminant, then no remediation can be required. If, however, there is such escape or the use of the land is to be changed, for example from industrial to residential, then remediation must be undertaken to ensure its suitability for that new use – and this will be a term of any planning consent for change of use, apart from any requirement by the enforcing authority.

There is power for the enforcing authority to compel remediation, and power too for the enforcing authority itself to clean up the land and charge the polluter (or in his absence the then owner/occupier) with the cost. However, it is central to the regime that remediation

[4] The enforcing authority will usually be the local authority.

50

will be undertaken voluntarily. This is evidenced by the fact that, save where there is imminent danger of serious harm or serious pollution of controlled waters, a minimum period of three months must elapse before the enforcing authority can serve a remediation notice. There is too a requirement for consultation with the person on whom it is intended to serve the notice as to the scope and method of remediation works to be undertaken.

Note that there is a potential conflict between the Contaminated Land Regulations and the Pollution Prevention and Control Regulations 2000 since each requires clean-up to a different standard. Moreover, PPC requires a contaminated land report to form part of the application for a PPC permit. It is too soon to tell whether the regulations will impact on property prices or whether there will be severe adverse consequences suffered by business directly as a result of the regulations. However, there is no doubt that there is an impact and that it will continue to be felt.

US WASTE REGULATION

The Resource Conservation and Recovery Act (RCRA) solid and hazardous waste regulations have had a marked influence on business. This section describes the history of RCRA, the role of the US EPA and the states, and hazardous waste definitions and management requirements, including the roles of generators and transporters, and treatment, storage and disposal facilities.

In 1965, to encourage environmentally sound methods for disposal of household, municipal, commercial and industrial refuse, Congress passed the first federal law to require safeguards on these activities, the Solid Waste Disposal Act. Congress amended this law in 1976 by passing the Resource Conservation and Recovery Act. Its primary goals are to:

- Protect human health and the environment from the potential hazards of waste disposal
- Conserve energy and natural resources
- Reduce the amount of waste generated
- Ensure that wastes are managed in an environmentally sound manner

As more information about health and environmental impacts of waste disposal became available, Congress revised RCRA in 1980 and again in 1984. The 1984 amendments are referred to as the Hazardous and Solid Waste Amendments.

RCRA is divided into sections called subtitles. Subtitles C and D and contain a framework for the EPA's comprehensive waste management programme:

- EPA's Subtitle C programme establishes a regulatory framework for managing hazardous waste from generation until ultimate disposal.
- EPA's Subtitle D programme establishes a system for managing solid (primarily non-hazardous) waste, such as household waste.

RCRA also regulates underground storage tanks (USTs) that store petroleum or certain chemical products under Subtitle I. Requirements exist for the design and operation of these tanks and the development of systems to prevent accidental spills. Examples of facilities using these tanks include petroleum refineries, chemical plants and commercial gas stations.

The Medical Waste Tracking Act 1988 was a two-year demonstration programme that expired in June 1991. It created a subtitle programme designed to track medical waste from generation to disposal. At present, no federal EPA tracking regulations are in force for medical waste, but many states have adopted their own programmes. CERCLA (see p. 48) is a related statute that deals with, among other things, cleaning up inactive and abandoned hazardous waste sites. RCRA, on the other hand, deals with materials that are currently destined for disposal or recycling. The term 'RCRA' is often used interchangeably to refer to the law, regulations and EPA

In any given state, the hazardous waste regulatory programme may be run by either EPA or a state hazardous waste agency. Both of these entities may be referred to as the 'regulatory agency', depending on the state. RCRA encourages states to assume primary responsibility for implementing the RCRA programme, instead of EPA. States that wish to adopt and implement the RCRA Subtitle C programme must develop a programme for the management of hazardous waste that is at least as stringent as the EPA programme. State programmes, as already noted however, can be more stringent or broader in scope. This process ensures that minimum standards are met nationwide, while providing flexibility to states in implementing rules, policy and guidance. The law describes the waste management programme mandated by Congress that gave EPA authority to develop the RCRA programme. EPA regulations carry out the congressional intent by providing explicit, legally enforceable requirements for waste management. These regulations are to be found in Title 40 of the Code of Federal Regulations (CFR), Parts 238 to 282. EPA guidance documents and policy directives clarify issues related to the implementation of the regulations. These three elements are the primary parts of the RCRA programme.

Proper management and disposal of hazardous wastes are essential to protect human health and the environment. RCRA provides a general definition of the term 'hazardous waste'. EPA has defined by regulation which specific materials are considered hazardous waste under Subtitle C. Under this definition, the universe of potential hazardous wastes is extremely large and diverse. The regulatory definition evolves and changes as new information becomes available. EPA works closely with industry and the public to determine which of these wastes should be subject to the RCRA hazardous waste regulations. EPA has developed four defining characteristics of hazardous waste and four lists of specific hazardous wastes.

According to one EPA estimate of the 13 billion US tons of industrial, agricultural, commercial and household wastes generated annually, more than 279 million US tons (2%) are 'hazardous', as defined by RCRA regulations (contrast this with the estimate on page 15).

EU WASTE REGULATION

Under the Treaty of Rome 1957, the Single European Act 1986 and the Treaty of Amsterdam, (which renumbered Articles 130r–t to Articles 174–176), there is now a proper and cogent framework for the implementation of environmental law throughout the EU. The 1975 Directive on Waste, the Waste Framework Directive 75/442/EC, as amended by Directives 91/156/EC and 91/692/EC, is the core piece of European legislation governing waste. It contains what has popularly become known as the Waste Hierarchy:

- The prevention or reduction of waste production and its harmfulness, particularly by the development of clean technologies
- The recovery of waste by means of recycling, reuse or reclamation or any other process with a view to extracting secondary raw materials
- The use of waste as a source of energy

Member states must establish competent authorities who must prepare waste disposal plans and regulate waste disposal undertakings by means of permits, inspections and other forms of supervision.

This core legislation is supplemented by the 1980 Directive on the Protection of Groundwater against Pollution Caused by Certain Dangerous Substances (80/68/EC), which bans or limits the introduction into groundwater of certain substances contained in the black (banned) and grey (limited) lists and by the 1984 Directive on the Combating of Air Pollution from Industrial Plant (84/360/EC) which requires a system of prior authorisation for some plant, including plant for the disposal of toxic and dangerous waste by incineration. Important to note too are the Hazardous Waste Directive (91/689/EC) controlling the disposal of hazardous wastes and the 1993 Regulation on the Supervision of and Control of Shipments of Waste 93/259/EC, which governs the transport of hazardous wastes by road, water or air across national boundaries and takes its authority from the Basel Convention on the Transboundary Movements of Hazardous Wastes and Their Disposal. The 1996 Integrated Pollution Prevention and Control Directive (96/61/EC) aims to achieve, among other things, the objective of avoiding waste production, or if that is not possible, recovering the waste, if that is economically feasible, and if it is not, then ensuring that it is disposed of in a manner to avoid impact on the environment.

Two further pieces of European legislation are worthy of note: the 1994 Packaging Waste Directive (94/62/EC), which aims to increase the use of reusable and recyclable packaging and sets targets to this end, and the Landfill Directive (1999/31/EC), which requires the amount of biodegradable waste going to landfill to be reduced substantially and sets targets for the accomplishment of that object.

CONCLUSION

This brief overview of salient pieces of EU and US environmental law demonstrates that there is more than one approach to the same problem and more than one solution. It is probably evident that in some instances the EU has borrowed legislative concepts from the United States, and vice versa. It is, however, also plain that legislation is not the complete answer to the degradation of the planet. Were it so, that degradation would be much reduced. As it is, it continues, with managers and others responsible for industry keen to avoid the rigours of the law without necessarily improving the environment. As will be seen though, industry may find itself agreeably surprised at the competitive edge that compliance, or compliance plus, may bring.

Photo: *Francesca Partridge.*

CHAPTER 3

Reputational Issues

INTRODUCTION

The first chapters of this book examined the changing external influences on business which are being brought about by environmental issues such as climate change and population growth and, of course, the emergence of the concept of sustainable development. Of rather more immediate concern, Chapter 2 examined the burgeoning subject of environmental law, which is witnessing an exponential growth in its scope and more recently in enforcement. This chapter examines a less tangible issue, reputation, from an environmental perspective and explores how the environment is, or should be, forcing businesses to examine how they present themselves.

But why should the environment, specifically, be worthy of consideration as a reputational issue? Currently, the most common approach to environmental problems, even disasters, is to pour cash into public relations and hope to keep the lid on until either the clean-up is complete or the media has found a more compelling interest. However, in common with most other things in life, the concept of reputation and, more importantly, how to preserve it, is changing. This change is driven by fundamental developments in the way business is being conducted.

The global economy has opened new markets, offered scope for reduced labour costs and offered year-round supply of hitherto seasonal products. However, on the other hand, with a head office in one country and a source of supply in another, there is a tendency for business leaders to lose sight of the impact their business has on local economies or, more importantly, on the hearts and minds of local populations. The communications revolution, which shows no sign of running out of steam, is another factor. Global communications are now cheap and plentiful and growing more so. Whether in the depths of the darkest and steamiest rainforests or in a city mall, pictures and opinion can be generated and disseminated in seconds, and reputations enhanced or damaged before the PR department can react to provide a company spin. The sheer size and scope of global businesses can also have an impact on the handling of reputational issues. The hundred largest companies have combined turnovers that are greater than the GDP of half the world's countries. In some cases the public consider it more appropriate to look to companies rather than to their government to protect their interests. This could be a positive factor in terms of image and reputation. However, given today's lack of deference to the previously unquestioned authority of governments and large businesses across the world, the local dominance of large corporations could be a double-edged sword. People are becoming more aware of the power in the laptop or mobile phone at their fingertips and are prepared to act in their own interests.

WHAT IS REPUTATION?

The purest treasure mortal times afford
Is spotless reputation; that away,
Men, are but gilded loam and painted clay.
(William Shakespeare, *Richard II*, Act I, scene 1)

A corporate reputation can be defined in various ways. It can be a representation of a company's ability to meet the expectation of its stakeholders. Equally, it can describe the rational and emotional attachments that stakeholders form with a company. Finally, and perhaps most familiarly, it can describe the net image a company develops with all of its stakeholders.

Although often used interchangeably, reputation is quite different from brand and image. A brand is a label that a business uses for its customers' benefit to distinguish it from its competitors. Brands can be applied to products, services or to the business as a whole. On the other hand, image is in the eye of the beholder and depends on the overall impact of the brand, product or service on an individual or group. It follows that image will depend on an individual's or group's personal values, experience and needs. A business can therefore have many images and brands but only one reputation. It is reputation, as Shakespeare recognised, that is important because it demonstrates the overall attractiveness of the business to all of its stakeholders, including employees, customers, investors, reporters and the public at large.

Reputation has always been a major factor in differentiating companies, and current business trends are likely to make reputation an increasingly important factor. For instance, the proliferation of information and advertising, whether in print or over the airwaves or the internet, can leave potential customers either spoilt for choice or, more likely, baffled as to the relative merits of competing products. Often reputation is the one factor upon which the confused or bemused customer feels he can depend to inform his choice of product or service. Reputation, too, can open doors to markets guarded by suspicious local governments, particularly where cultural divides need to be bridged.

Finally, although difficult to prove, there is empirical evidence to suggest that a good reputation helps a business to become an employer of first choice, particularly for top graduates. Similarly, working within a business with a good reputation is likely to be a factor in retaining top performers.

STAKEHOLDERS

In 1995 the Royal Society of Arts, Manufacturing and Commerce published the findings of its inquiry into tomorrow's company. On change, the inquiry's chairman, Sir Anthony Cleaver, stated that almost everything about a company over a period of time can change: the products it makes, the markets it serves, the geography in which it operates, the technology which it employs, its manufacturing processes and raw materials. However, he went on to claim that the one thing that does not change within a company is its five key stakeholders:

- Its shareholders
- Its employees

- Its customers
- Its suppliers and partners
- The community at large

Within the 'community at large' can be identified a further set of important relationships:

- Governments and regulators
- Social and environmental pressure groups
- The media and academia
- Trade bodies
- Competitors

The expectations of stakeholders differ. Historically, the short-term returns, in terms of dividends and share value, of shareholders have been given priority over the wider interests of other stakeholders. Increasingly, this approach is being seen to be in conflict with expectations for more socially and environmentally sensitive policies and has exposed companies to censure, particularly by customers and the wider community (this may be especially true in a country such as the UK where, compared to the US, large sections of society have only recently been exposed to share ownership).

For instance, in a celebrated case in 1995 Shell focused on the legislative aspects of disposing of its huge Brent Spar oil storage rig. Having assured itself that it would be compliant with all relevant legislation, Shell decided that the best environmental option was to scuttle the rig in the North Sea. Environmental activists protested vigorously but Shell paid no heed, it was content that its case was logical and therefore unassailable. Greenpeace released a torrent of publicity against Shell, based on what later proved to be an incorrect analysis of the environmental impact of sinking the Brent Spar. Nevertheless, Greenpeace's onslaught served to bring the proposal to the attention of the public so successfully that Shell had to back down in the face of public outrage demonstrated by a successful boycott of its products in Germany. Also in 1995, Shell's reputation was further dented when the military government of Nigeria executed Ken Saro-Wiwa and eight other environmental activists on what was believed by many international governments to be dubious evidence and after an unfair trial. Saro-Wiwa's 'crime' had been to encourage his fellow Ogoni people to protest about the impact of more than thirty years of exploitation of their land by Shell.

The relationship with particular stakeholders will vary with time and circumstances, with potentially dire consequences for reputations. At the local level, the expectations of the local community, which might focus on jobs, amenity facilities and less pollution, are often at odds with those of head office, which is likely to see the situation in quite different terms. Although local populations can rarely expect to influence company policy or strategy due to their lack of voice, geographical remoteness or because of their fragmented organisation, sometimes, as the Shell examples demonstrate, the balance can be redressed by the intervention of pressure groups such as Greenpeace and by the media. One way or another, stakeholders are becoming more aware of their power and are not prepared to hold their peace. An example of how the effects of a disaster can continue for many years is demonstrated by the Bhopal incident in India.

On 2 December 1984 a leak at the Union Carbide pesticide plant in Bhopal, released a cloud of toxic gas which caused about 4,000 deaths and injured thousands more. Although Union Carbide agreed to pay compensation to the victims and their families and to build a hospital, many Indians thought that the company had paid substantially less than it would have had to pay had the accident happened in the United States. In 1988 Union Carbide's chairman admitted:

> [In the 1970s] our safety record was unequalled among manufacturers. Our employees were healthier than most people, and we were aggressively establishing ourselves competitively in the markets of the world. Then, in few short years, our world seemed to change. Today, we are one of the most feared and misunderstood industries in the history of the planet. (M. McIntosh, D. Leipziger, K. Jones and G. Coleman, 1998, *Corporate Citizenship*, FT Pitman Publishing, p. 69)

In August 2000 Greenpeace reported that the suffering of the gas victims living around the now abandoned factory site was being aggravated by the presence of several tons of toxic wastes that were lying scattered and exposed to the environment within the

61

factory premises. The remaining victims endeavoured to gain compensation, medical relief and economic rehabilitation. On 6 February 2001 Union Carbide merged with Dow Chemical International to create one of the largest chemical companies in the world. However, currently there seems little hope that the Bhopal victims and their support groups would release Union Carbide from what they maintained were its obligations. Accordingly, a group of survivors picketed the Dow office at Corporate Park, Bombay, to present a memorandum requiring Dow to accept Union Carbide's liabilities incurred at Bhopal. Apparently, Dow staff initially refused to accept the memorandum, claiming that they were nothing to do with Union Carbide, which added credence to the survivors' concern that 'by becoming a Dow subsidiary, Union Carbide is seeking to shake off its hated name'. However, eventually they delivered their document and left with the promise that Dow would meet them to discuss their demands. Meanwhile, the survivors' leaders announced that the Bhopal campaign would go on but that the focus would be transferred to Dow.

One organisation that has learned to identify its key stakeholders and to engage them pre-emptively is the Royal Air Force (RAF). The RAF perceives a need to carry out flying training at low level in order to maintain its operational effectiveness. The sight and sound of large and noisy aircraft skimming over some of the UK's most scenically spectacular countryside has never been universally popular. However, the RAF has kept one step ahead of the counter-arguments by dint of a strongly argued operational case and engagement of stakeholders at all levels. In the mid 1990s the low-level flying issue was brought to a head in Germany when evidence was assembled that linked the impact of low flying by the Luftwaffe and other allied air forces with problems in the cognitive development of children. All military jet low flying in Germany was stopped as a result.

In the UK the RAF marshalled its scientific resources to review the German evidence against low flying and determined that it was flawed. It then launched an effective campaign on several fronts to head off the forthcoming campaign against low flying in the UK. First, it argued its case within the scientific community by presenting papers on the low-level flying health issue to peers at conferences.

Secondly, it invited every Member of Parliament to a high-level briefing on the RAF's interpretation of the German evidence and of its continuing need to fly at low level. This effectively prevented the issue from being argued out on the floor of the House of Commons with attendant poor publicity and wider coverage by the media and pressure groups. Thirdly, it armed its PR department with the facts as it saw them. So far, the RAF continues to enjoy a mandate to fly at low level in the UK.

The Shell example illustrates how easy it is on the one hand to damage a reputation, perhaps unfairly, by overlooking or ignoring vital stakeholders. On the other hand, the RAF, which did not want to fight and probably lose the low-flying debate on ground not of its choosing, identified its critical stakeholders and fought successfully from a position of strength. The RAF example also highlights the need to identify key stakeholders for specific issues and to prepare individual approaches to them to achieve the most productive relationship. One technique for this is stakeholder mapping, a process whereby the company identifies its stakeholders and the most effective means of communication with them. This often requires some lateral thinking, as some stakeholders may not be immediately obvious to the company and neither will the company be able to judge the nature of the relationship necessary to communicate with them.

MAKING A CORPORATE COMMITMENT

Most governments in the developed world, and an increasing number in the developing world, recognise that sustainable development, with its focus on good environmental performance, is an issue where business and government must work together. Traditionally, governments have been content to regulate environmental performance through legislation and the threat of prosecution; however, the situation is changing and governments are developing various means to spur improved environmental performance. As we have seen (p. 38), in Europe the 1957 Treaty of Rome, which created the European Economic Community, did not address the environment at all. The Single European Act of 1986 however adopted specific environmental objectives:

- To preserve, protect and improve the quality of the environment
- To contribute towards protecting human health
- To ensure a prudent and rational utilisation of natural resources

As we have seen too, these objectives were extended by the Treaty of the European Union 1992, the Maastricht treaty, to include:

- Sustainable and non-inflationary growth respecting the environment
- Promotion of measures to help resolve global environmental problems

The above developments in the legal and policy context within the EU are already having an effect on the conduct of business. In the UK, developments in pension legislation (Chapter 5) require fund managers to report on how they take environmental considerations into account in their investments. Ultimately, this is likely to provide companies with positive or negative reputations concerning the environment, whether they like it or not. Moreover, it would appear logical to assume that those with a poor reputation in this area will be sidelined. The *UK Company Law Review* recently addressed the possibility of greater disclosure about environmental performance, and while its current conclusion is not to recommend a change in the law, over time this may change. Against this background, the UK has recently implemented two measures that are designed to encourage improvements in environmental performance and, moreover, to bring good and bad performers to public notice.

In 1991 the UK government launched Making a Corporate Commitment (MACC). Relaunched in 1999 as one of several initiatives stemming from the UK government's Sustainable Development Strategy published in that year, MACC 2 requires companies to set quantified targets for improving resource efficiency and environmental performance (*Making a Corporate Commitment*, DETR). Significantly, it also requires targets to be reported. MACC 2 is a voluntary mechanism equally suited to businesses and the public sector, whether or not they already have environmental management systems. Specifically, to take part in MACC 2, organisations need to declare targets for reductions in at least one (and preferably more) of the following areas: greenhouse gas emissions, waste production and water use. These are commonly regarded as key measures of resource efficiency and can be readily identified. MACC 2 also encourages reporting of environmental initiatives in other areas such as company travel planning, encouragement of biodiversity, raw material use or emissions of non-greenhouse gases.

MACC 2 claims there are several advantages awaiting businesses that join the programme. First, it clearly demonstrates a top-level commitment and marks out participating businesses as being visionaries and sector leaders. Secondly, MACC 2 provides a mechanism for meeting the demands for greater openness in the conduct of business. It also encourages organisations to examine the way they employ resources, which is an acknowledged first step on the road to making bottom line savings.

Signatories to MACC 2 are listed on the MACC 2 website (www.macc2.org.uk), which clearly makes the commitment public. Take-up was expected to be gradual in the early stages, given the need for businesses to select data sets and create baselines against which to measure performance. However, the UK minister for the environment has written in uncompromising terms to all chief executives, or equivalents, of nearly 10,000 organisations in the UK which employ more than 250 staff, exhorting them to sign up to MACC 2. Early commitments were received from a cross-section of the business and public sectors, including:

- British Airways
- British Telecommunications plc
- Corporation of London
- Financial Services Authority
- RJB Mining
- Rio Tinto
- Rolls-Royce Navy Marine Operations
- Safeway
- Sainsbury's

The UK government is keen to promote environmental reporting as the prime minister made clear during a speech to the Confederation of British Industry/Green Alliance Conference on the Environment on 24 October 2000:

The pioneers of environmental reporting are seeing increasing benefits from both improved efficiencies and public image as a result. This is something that all companies should be doing, and I am issuing a challenge, today, to all of the top 350 companies to be publishing annual environment reports by the end of 2001.

The second example, within the UK, where reputation is being used as a measure to help ensure good environmental performance is the annual Business Environmental Performance Report published by the Environment Agency (EA), the main environmental regulator for England and Wales. The EA believes that environmental protection can be delivered through a range of measures, including regulation, economic incentives, education and voluntary measures (Spotlight on Business Environmental Performance, Environment Agency). It also considers that reporting on the performance of the industries that it regulates is a powerful incentive for them to take greater responsibility for their environmental performance. First introduced in 1998, the business performance report was conceived as a 'name and shame' report on businesses that had been fined for pollution offences; this was not dissimilar to the approach taken by the US EPA, which publishes a comprehensive list of offenders on its website.

In its second report, the EA provided the carrot as well as the stick by providing two league tables, one of good performers that have reduced the amount of pollution they produce and the other of poor performers that have been fined and prosecuted for pollution offences. The EA maintains it is providing this information because it wants businesses and those who finance their activities to ensure that environmental improvements are delivered. It goes on to stress that all companies should provide environmental information in their annual reports and accounts for their shareholders, staff and customers and, where appropriate, produce environmental reports. The EA also emphasises that its stand on reporting is consistent with the new pension fund regulations and with proposals in the company law review. The EA recognises that it needs to develop further its methods for measuring environmental performance and that to do this it will need to open a dialogue with industry.

It is too early to say how effective MACC 2 and the annual EA Business Environmental Performance Report will be. However, it seems clear that there is an increasing willingness within the UK government to focus on reputations as a means to persuade industry to clean up and improve its environmental act. No doubt, too, these two measures will also provide another source of information for investors and fund managers.

REPUTATION AND SHAREHOLDER ACTIVISM

Shareholder activism first emerged in the US following the Wall Street crash of the late 1920s, which many shareholders blamed, in part at any rate, on a lack of openness among US listed companies. Since then the focus of shareholder activism has moved on from issues such as commercial transparency and traditional and some-what selfish concepts of investor protection. In the 1970s, the Viet-nam War and the emergence of the military/industrial complex prompted disquiet in some circles at the developments of an overly cosy relationship between the military and industry during the prosecution of a costly and unpopular war. Later, apartheid in South Africa caused many investors to question whether profit should be the only driver for business and the only measure of success. In the 1980s and 1990s, growing social awareness among shareholders, particularly in view of the globalisation of markets and concerns about such issues as the environment, child labour and sweatshop conditions, led some to question whether the bond of accountability between directors and shareholders had broken down.

Shareholder activism is still a mainly US phenomenon due to the relative ease with which resolutions can be lodged in the US. In the UK, for instance, the law requires a minimum level of shareholding before a resolution can be proposed to an annual general meeting (AGM), which makes such action difficult, time-consuming and expensive to arrange (Andrew White, *Elements*, March 2001, pp. 10–12). In 1999 over 220 resolutions raising concern over environ-mental and social performance were filed with over 150 large US companies, and many of these resolutions gained between 10% and 20% of the total vote on each proposal. In the US, shareholders have realised that activism, even by minorities, is a potent means to influence corporate policy. After all, few directors wish to see the hijacking of AGM agendas with attendant possibilities for unwelcome media interest and public scrutiny. Examples of some of these resolutions and their results are given in Chapter 6.

Within Europe, UK shareholders appear to be particularly alive to the possibilities afforded by activism, and minorities have shown themselves willing and able to punch above their weight. For instance, in 1997 shareholders in Shell Transport and Trading, the minority partner in Royal Dutch/Shell Group, the world's second-largest oil and gas company, lodged a motion on social auditing at the company AGM. Although the motion was defeated, the shareholder action was a significant factor in causing Shell to change its approach to corporate responsibility issues.

A significant factor in the evolution of shareholder activism is the willingness of pressure groups such as Greenpeace, which is more usually associated with sensational and high-profile campaigns on the high seas, to achieve their aims via the resolution route. Greenpeace is currently engaging with BP on a range of issues that serve as a good example of how reputations can be attacked from unexpected directions. In 1999 Greenpeace, the US Public Research Interest Group and individual investors came together under an umbrella organisation called SANEBP (Shareholders Against New Oil Exploration). SANEBP's stated aim was to work for an end to new oil exploration by BP and a redirection of investment into renewable energy markets. It claimed to offer intelligence, advice and encouragement to BP shareholders wishing to move the company away from reliance on fossil fuels and towards a future in renewable energy. Along with US ethical investor Trillium Asset Management, SANEBP put forward a resolution to the BP AGM on 13 April 2000 to:

• Cancel all plans for oil exploration and development on the coastal plain of the Arctic National Wildlife Refuge and in the Arctic Ocean.
• Stop the expenditure of any funds by the company or its subsidiary or associate companies targeted to achieve these objectives, including investments of the Northstar project (the extraction of Arctic oil).

- Make capital freed up by the cancellation of Northstar available to BP Solarex to enhance its solar manufacturing capacity.

In the event, 1,491,140,205 shares voted in favour of the resolution. This represented 13.5% of the vote, with a share value of £8 billion – in SANEBP's view an unprecedented result for a resolution of this kind.

Keeping the pressure on BP, SANEBP reminded shareholders that they owned the company and could influence the way in which it was run. Moreover, a large part of UK company law existed to prevent shareholders' interests from being abused by the company. It then contended that the strategic direction taken by the company was not consistent with BP's public stance on the need for precautionary action on climate change. Moreover, it pointed out that in any case BP's current policy did not take account of potential climate change measures that were likely to restrict the production and sale of fossil fuels. Pressing this point, SANEBP pointed to BP's much proclaimed rebranding during which, in September 2000, BP's chairman, Lord Browne, stated that the initials BP would in future stand for 'Beyond Petroleum'.

In early 2001 SANEBP pressed BP to be more specific about its plans to 'move beyond petroleum' and prepared a resolution for BP's AGM to this effect. The text of the resolution stated:

In recognition of:

- The business risk and threat to the environment, particularly from global warming, linked to the production and use of fossil fuels;

- The associated business opportunities for involvement in alternative or renewable energy production;

- The Company's commitment to environmental responsibility and the targets already set by the Company to reduce its internal greenhouse gas emissions.

The Directors are hereby directed to prepare, publish and circulate to shareholders a report by the end of 2001 setting out a strategy for going 'beyond petroleum' for reducing and eventually phasing out the production and sale of fossil fuels in response to climate change. The report shall include quantified targets and clear timescales for:

- Absolute reductions in aggregate greenhouse gas emissions associated with the group's operations and products;

- Investment in renewable energy as a proportion of overall group investment; and

- Changes in the composition of the group's energy production to reduce and eventually phase out its production and sale of fossil fuels.

Originally, the resolution was framed as an ordinary resolution, which could be carried by a simple majority, 'requesting' BP's directors to prepare a strategy for 'going beyond petroleum'. However, BP insisted that the resolution be reworded to 'direct' the preparation of the report and thus to require it to be framed as a special resolution. In effect, the resolution became a direct challenge to the board and ensured that the resolution stood no chance of gaining the 75% of the vote required to carry it.

Margo Dunn, chair of the staffing committee at the London Borough of Islington, one of the co-sponsors of the resolution, was quoted by SANEBP as saying, 'I am saddened that BP Amoco feels so threatened that they're forcing Greenpeace to use a Special Resolution. If they are so convinced in their own minds that they are doing the everything possible to "go beyond petroleum", why are they afraid of this rather gentle prod in the right direction?'

BP, in common with other oil companies such as Chevron, Exxon-Mobil and Shell, has been trying to create a reputation as a green and forward-looking company under a chairman who has gained a reputation as a businessman who recognises the need to work in harmony with the environment. However, Greenpeace identified what they maintained were inconsistencies in the BP approach, but there were few options open to Greenpeace to take direct action and bring their grievance to wider notice, as they did during the Shell Brent Spar campaign. This time, Greenpeace recognised that shareholder activism was likely to be the most effective means to achieve their aims. The 2000 resolution made relatively few waves outside the BP shareholder community. Yet undoubtedly it will have served as a wake-up call to many shareholders who will have realised that the reputation of their company was under a determined assault. The 2001 resolution will be put before BP's shareholders after a period when the company's credibility in the UK on safety and environmental matters has diminished in light of several breaches of legal standards over the past two years (*ENDS Report*, No. 308, p. 3).

At BP's Grangemouth oil refinery there were a series of incidents, including breaches of oil discharge limits, and BP itself reported a 24% increase in discharges of pollutants and a fourfold increase in oil spills. There was also an accidental flaring of excess gas, which led to smoke emissions and significant concerns among the local population. Local concerns were also raised after a burst steam pipe made a 'noise like a jumbo jet taking off' and, three days later, a major fire required use of on-site and public fire services to bring it under control. Public sentiment about the Grangemouth refinery was summed up by a local government councillor who was quoted in BP's environmental report; the councillor 'was profoundly upset by recurrent incidents at the Grangemouth plant that leave us fearing for our safety'. Other unpleasant incidents were recorded at BP's Coryton refinery in Essex and on the River Tweed, when overfilling of a fuel tank caused oil pollution and a fine of £15,000 plus £200,000 in clean-up costs.

Perhaps the worst incident from a reputational perspective was the withdrawal of certification of the Sullom Voe site's registration under the European Eco-Management and Audit Scheme (EMAS) after a number of environmental incidents recorded by the Scottish Environmental Protection Agency. (The Scottish Environmental Protection Agency is the Scottish equivalent of the English Environment Agency and is the main environmental regulator for Scotland.) Although the EMAS registration was subsequently restored following prompt corrective action, the company had to suffer the indignity of being the first organisation in the UK to have its registration withdrawn.

71

BP's environmental reputation has been examined at some length as it illustrates the problem of matching performance to rhetoric in a way that satisfies the increasing body of sceptical and determined activists who, it appears, genuinely believe that big business should lead the way in terms of environmental performance. What is even more interesting is that Greenpeace's concerns over the strategic direction being taken by the company appear to be shared by a significant minority of BP's shareholders. Add to these the stakeholders who have experienced first-hand some of BP's more obvious environmental problems, and BP's environmental reputation could be set to suffer. Perhaps the lesson emerging from BP's rough treatment at the hands of stakeholder activists is that businesses must avoid 'greenwash', long used as a derogative term within environmental circles to describe overly optimistic claims for environmental performance. After all, the term has recently been taken into the official lexicon of the English language, The tenth edition of the *Concise Oxford English Dictionary* defines 'greenwash' as 'disinformation disseminated by an organisation so as to present an environmentally responsible public image'.

REPUTATION AND STRATEGIC PARTNERSHIP

Although in different industries, McDonald's and BP have certain features in common. Both have a global presence; both deal in commodities that arouse strong passions due to their impact on the environment; and both have come under strong attack by environmental activists. In McDonald's case, though, activism that could have sullied its reputation irredeemably was the spur to improve its environmental performance and to enhance its reputation as well.

In 1989 McDonald's was coming under increasing pressure from several directions for what was perceived to be its uncaring approach to environmental issues, particularly waste. With few organisations willing to work with them, the company was at a loss how to proceed until Ed Rensi, president of McDonald's USA, took up an invitation from the Environmental Defence Fund and met its executive director, Fred Krupp. EDF was founded in 1967 with a grant from the Rachel

Carson Memorial Fund to fight the use of DDT. Fred Krupp, a Harvard lawyer, improved EDF's scientific and technical capabilities and developed it into a highly professional group specialising in market-based solutions to business problems. Krupp maintained that environmentalists could become more influential and effective if they employed a wider variety of tactics. His approach was aggressively to lobby, litigate and criticise poor corporate environmental performance and to promote stricter regulation. Significantly, though, he also saw a need to problem-solve with corporations. With its headquarters in New York City, EDF has seven offices in the US, a professional staff of over 110 scientists, economists, attorneys, engineers and administrators and receives support from more than 200,000 members and over 100 private foundations.

In 1990, to the surprise of many, McDonald's and EDF joined forces in a collaborative project, the Waste Reduction Task Force. In the first effort of its kind, America's largest quick-service restaurant business and one of the country's leading environmental research and advocacy organisations worked together to determine ways to reduce McDonald's solid waste through source reduction, reuse, recycling and composting. In undertaking this project, McDonald's committed itself to an unprecedented level of scrutiny by an outside organisation.

The McDonald's–EDF alliance has been in operation for over a decade. Total waste savings and increases in the use of recycled material, all of which are verified by EDF, have been considerable although this has been achieved by incremental changes to materials and processes rather than dramatic breakthroughs, as the following list suggests:

1990   reduced thickness of sundae cups
1991   reduced size of napkins by one inch
1992   reduced basis weight of Happy Meal bag
1993   reduced back flap of fry carton
1994   reduced thickness of trash can liners
1995   replaced hash brown cartons with bags
1996   changed to thinner carry-out bags
1997   decreased weight of in-store trays
1998   converted to sandwich wraps for fish sandwich
1999   introduced insulated wraps for Quarter Pounder sandwich

While some would say that the alliance with EDF has merely provided an excellent source of PR for McDonald's, they miss the point. Any business requires a mandate from its stakeholders to continue in business. McDonald's recognised this and knew that its business, with its highly visible output of waste, would become increasingly difficult to justify. It therefore seized the opportunity to guard its reputation and maintain its position as a leader in the fast food market.

REPUTATION AND THE UNTHINKABLE

So far this chapter has addressed reputation as a significant but positive factor in business. Unfortunately, the reverse is true too; reputations can turn bad over long periods, reflecting the natural death of a business. However, there are relatively rare instances where companies fail to rise to a challenge and reputation becomes an instant make or break issue. Two tragic cases illustrate the point.

One night in 1987 the Townsend Thorenson car ferry *Herald of Free Enterprise* set off from Zeebrugge in Holland to return to her home port of Dover in England. Slightly behind schedule, the ferry departed with her bow doors open, a not uncommon practice at the time. Minutes after leaving harbour and with the condition of the bow doors apparently forgotten, the ship increased speed, water flooded the ship's vehicle deck through the open doors and she keeled over. Despite being only half submerged and within sight of the harbour, 193 people died. It took three days before a senior Townsend Thorensen manager agreed to be interviewed about the disaster.

In 1989 a total of 47 passengers died when a British Midland Boeing 737 crashed at Kegworth near one of the UK's regional airports. In contrast to Townsend Thorenson, British Midland responded immediately and a senior manager was quickly on site to represent the company. British Midland was prepared to personalise the disaster and to demonstrate responsibility without prejudice to issues of causation. Townsend Thorenson missed the opportunity. British Midland survived, Townsend Thorenson did not.

CONCLUSION

A strong and readily identifiable reputation is always a good asset. However, a poor reputation can be disastrous. Businesses must earn their 'licence or mandate to operate', which means that stakeholder confidence must be maintained. As the examples in this chapter have shown, businesses which allow any undermining of their licences to operate, by their own actions or omissions or by those of activists, expose themselves to a range of sanctions.

In the past, business reputations mainly rested on producing the right product at the right price at the right time and with repeatable quality. However, today's business environment is far more complex than even a decade ago. Markets have expanded to cover the globe and exposed businesses to new stakeholders from a vast range of cultural and economic backgrounds who may not appreciate the motives and ethos of businesses located on the far side of the globe. Standards too are changing, driven by advances in technology, and with rising standards come increased expectations concerning issues such as efficient use of natural resources, pollution and waste. Companies that are seen to be insensitive to these developments run an increasing risk of finding themselves the target of not only environmental regulators and the media, but also highly organised and effective campaigners. Worse, modern communications can ensure that bad publicity reaches and perhaps influences a global audience almost instantly.

It has been said that a reputation can take twenty years to build and twenty minutes to destroy. This may be true, but it need not necessarily be so. Reputation is highly important and should receive top-level management attention. Often it is assumed that a good reputation is the inevitable consequence of the total efforts of well-run sales, quality and PR departments. However, the examples in this chapter indicate that serious threats to reputation and business success often emerge from unexpected directions and that these are unlikely to be covered by any one department. From these, a few basic dos and don'ts regarding reputation can be assembled:

- *Stakeholder dialogue*: stakeholders should be identified and channels of communication established. It is vitally important to understand what interests, motivates and excites a company's

75

many and varied stakeholders. This is not a PR issue as most of the communication should be inwards.

- *Keep an eye on the ball*: having established a dialogue with stakeholders, companies should be careful to act upon the concerns expressed by them and be sensitive to changes in their concerns.
- *Open and honest communication*: as the BP case study illustrates, failure to match rhetoric with reality, particularly where market or sector leadership is being implied, invites criticism. In the past this might have been confined to the raucous complaints of a vociferous minority. However, today's activists are as likely to be at the AGM dressed in collar and tie as on the streets in boots and anorak.
- *Good intentions must be complemented by evidence*: the public does not naturally warm to large companies, particularly if they are from another country and culture. Therefore, it is important that companies setting out to convince stakeholders of the benefits of new strategies, operations or developments of existing products should have evidence of action plans and the necessary resources to hand. If necessary, evidence should be complemented by third-party verification.
- *Avoid covering up failure*: inevitably, not all initiatives will be successful and it is important to a company's credibility to be open and honest about failures. While BP has suffered some embarrassing failures in the environmental management at some of its sites in the UK, it has confronted each problem with commendable openness.

PART II

The Corporate Response

CHAPTER 4

Environmental Accounting and Reporting

INTRODUCTION

Most companies use accounting systems that were designed before the importance of environmental costs and impacts came to be understood. Until the 1990s, environmental compliance costs and environmental impacts caused by company activities were neither easy nor cost-effective for most companies to monitor; what is more, companies had little desire to do so. That is now changing; the growing use of environmental management systems, the expansion use of the polluter pays principle, and the desire of an investor to understand what is happening within the company in which it invests have conspired together to initiate a quiet revolution. However, it is still the case that an investor, actual or potential, may not always find it easy to identify the environmental principles of a company or the environmental spend which gives them substance. This chapter takes a hard look at what is available to assist the investor and examines how financial accounting and management accounting is, or can be, employed to identify the real environmental performance of a company. We look too at how companies report their environmental performance. Environmental accounting and reporting are usually considered as a single topic. However, in this chapter the issues are considered separately because, while there are mandatory requirements covering accounting for all expenditure, including environmental expenditure, there are as yet no equivalent stipulations for environmental reporting.

Although the two are often juxtaposed, there is a distinct difference between financial accounting and management accounting. Financial accounting is a standardised means for compiling and communicating financial information to external audiences—in effect, a scorekeeping and reporting tool. Management accounting is a means of supplying information to help managers plan and control organisational activities and to evaluate performance. The information gathered can be limited, for example, to financial data used to gauge profitability or extended to provide information on environmental performance. Collation of environmental data is often achieved through an environmental management system (Chapter 7) which provides for the identification, monitoring, and reporting of corporate environmental impacts, and for the integration of those impacts into corporate decisions on product costing, product pricing, capital budgeting, product design, and performance evaluation.

If the information once collected is to be made available for public use then the company must carefully consider for what segment of the public the information is primarily intended. As discussed earlier society has entrusted the management of a large portion of its wealth to corporate management. As a result, corporation executives become responsible to numerous internal and external stakeholders. Owners of the company (shareholders) are the immediate audience. Owners' interest is in the status of assets and the performance of the business. Shareholders seek to ensure that the company is protected against environmental liabilities. Expanding owners' interest into meeting legal environmental obligations brings an extended audience: consumers, competition, courts and legal system, employees, financial institutions, general public, government, interest groups, media, scientific community, and suppliers. This extended audience has a varied appetite for environmental reporting of business activities (E. Freeman, 1984, *Strategic Management: A Stakeholder Approach*, Pitman).

There is no easy way to identify the environmental spend. There are any number of different bodies, international and national, governmental and private, that have attempted to prepare rules for classification of different types of expenditure and their application. And in the same way, it will be seen that there are different ways of treating socially responsible investment:

- *Negative screen*: reject as investees those companies whose business lies in smoking, drinking or gambling
- *Positive screen*: support companies which seem responsive to change

So there are different ways of viewing the environmental spend:

- Negatively and reactively in response to external pressure
- Positively and proactively to achieve a standard higher than mere compliance and which results in a competitive advantage

THE EMERGENCE OF ENVIRONMENTAL ACCOUNTING

The purpose of financial accounting and reporting is to generate financial information about a company in order to provide a basis for transparency and accountability in relationships with stakeholders such as shareholders. Remember that financial information when published is historic and represents the point in time in the life of the company when the data was extracted. Financial reporting is used by managers to communicate the dated financial information to external parties. Information reported reflects the financial position as at a certain date and the changes in financial position since the date of the previous report.

Over time, standard-setting bodies and regulatory agencies have been established to try to make sure that necessary information is supplied to stakeholders in an unbiased way. Financial reporting systems use standardised conventions about how to treat specific items. A company applying standards and conventions assists the stakeholder with its accountability and decision-making needs. Professional financial auditors review company accounting information and financial reports for compliance with company law requirements and financial reporting and accountancy standards, thereby maintaining credibility of the reported information and the public reporting process. Financial reporting and accounting

standards influence a company's decision on what type of information is collected, how it is recorded, and then analysed and considered for disclosure. According to the International Accounting
Standards Committee (IASC), 'the objective of financial statements
is to provide information about the financial position, performance
and changes in the financial position of an enterprise that is useful
to a wide range of users in making economic decisions'. Of course
these objectives will be influenced by changes in the economic,
legal, political and social environment (Figure 4.1).

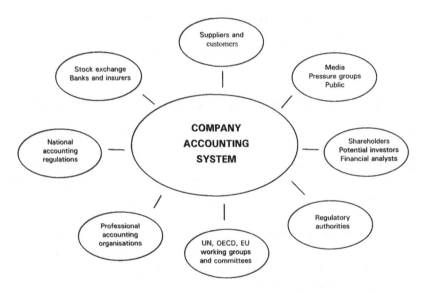

Figure 4.1 *Stakeholder and other influences on company accounting systems*

The accounting standards and regulations properly applied should
ultimately help with stakeholder decision-making and serve the
wider public interest by providing even-handed information to
support an efficient functioning of capital and other markets. And
remember that financial reports should give a true and fair view of
the financial position of the company and be externally verifiable if
they are to be useful. However, the effectiveness of given information
varies with time and changes in the wider environment. Thus,

accounting standards need to be regularly reviewed and updated where necessary to ensure appropriate reporting in an ever changing world.

As the environmental temperature has risen, so stakeholders have begun to enquire into the environmental performance of companies. If the stakeholder is a banker or financial analyst, the first examination will be of the company report and accounts. There has been much debate as to whether existing financial standards are adequate to provide for environmental accounting and reporting. However, legislation, regulation and standards which bear on how a company chooses, or is obliged, to report already provide mechanisms for examining environmental performance:

- Balance sheet provisions for liabilities and risks
- Estimation of the amount of a contingency
- Provision for long-term decommissioning costs
- Capitalisation of costs
- Offsetting of liabilities and expected recoveries
- Asset impairment and provision for repair costs

In addition SAS (Statement of Auditing Standard, published by the UK Accounting Standards Board) No. 120 (SAS 120) impacts on work professional financial auditors (auditors) must carry out with respect to an audit. The standard indicates that auditors must 'plan and perform their audit procedures and evaluate and report on the results thereof, recognising that non-compliance by the entity with law or regulations may materially affect the financial statements' (SAS 120.1).

In practice this should mean that the auditors must:

- Gain a general understanding of the legal and regulatory framework applicable both to the company and the industry of which the company forms part
- Look at the procedures followed to ensure compliance with the framework
- Inspect correspondence with relevant licensing or regulatory authorities
- Enquire of the directors as to whether they are on notice of any possible instances of non-compliance with law or regulations

- Obtain written confirmation from the directors that they have disclosed all the events of which they are aware which involve possible non-compliance together with actual and/or contingent consequences which may arise therefrom
- Consider the implications of suspected or actual non-compliance and document their findings

SAS 120 states that where auditors conclude that a suspected or actual instance of non-compliance with law or regulation has a material effect on the financial statements and they disagree with the accounting treatment or with the extent of or the lack of any disclosure of the instance or its consequences, they should issue an adverse or qualified report. Moreover, if the auditors become aware of a suspected or actual non-compliance with law or regulation which gives rise to a statutory duty to report—an example of this is the commission of an environmental offence for which the sanctions are criminal—then the report should be made without undue delay (but the auditors may first discuss their findings with the company). The position is different, however, if the auditors, because of the suspected or actual instance of non-compliance, no longer have confidence in the integrity of the directors. In those circumstances the auditors should report the matter direct to the proper authority in the public interest and without discussing it with the company.

Directors, or those to whom the function is delegated, must be satisfied that they are able to provide the auditors with the information to enable them to discharge their duties under SAS 120. The following items may be relevant:

- Maintaining an up-to-date register of relevant legislation and regulation
- Monitoring legal requirements and changes in them and ensuring that operating procedures are designed to meet those requirements
- Instilling and operating appropriate systems of internal control
- Developing a code of conduct ensuring employees are properly trained in and understand its provisions, monitoring compliance and taking appropriate disciplinary action

In public companies it is expected that these policies and procedures may be supplemented by assigning appropriate responsibilities to the relevant group for example, internal audit, legal, compliance, or the audit committee.

Lastly it should be noted that from the directors' and officers' perspective, there is a duty under section 389A(1) of the Companies Act 1985 to provide information required by the auditors to which they may have a legal right of access and that giving auditors information or explanations which are misleading, false or deceptive is a criminal offence.

Thus it might be argued that there is no need for specific regulations to govern environmental aspects—all are already catered for. However, the growing number of environmental issues, such as contaminated land, pollution prevention, waste management with its associated landfill problems, and perhaps most importantly climate change issues, which have resulted in the climate change levy, pose substantial financial consequences for companies. In light of this, stakeholders have sought to press standard-setting bodies and regulators to create new reporting standards regulations and guidelines specifically addressing environmental matters.

ENVIRONMENTAL ISSUES IN FINANCIAL ACCOUNTING

According to Roger Adams, head of technical services and research at ACCA, investors require assurance that a company is meeting all necessary obligations arising from its stated environmental and social policies. They need to know that a company manages its operations in such a way that it meets relevant legal regulations and minimises its exposure to any potential environmental liabilities. Companies adopt different mechanisms to provide assurances required as to future liability and risk. These mechanisms can include accreditation under internationally recognised management systems standards such as ISO 14000 and the EMAS.

The main environmental topics in company financial accounting are the recognition, measurement and disclosure of environmentally related economic impacts on business and the differentiation between capital expenditure and revenue items; each will be looked at in turn.

Recognition

The Accounting Standards Board issues Financial Reporting Standards and under FRS 12 a provision should be recognised when an entity has a legal and constructive obligation to transfer economic benefits as a result of past events. It will be noted that there are three limbs to the test, all of which must be satisfied:

- A present obligation as a result of a past event
- An obligation to transfer economic benefits
- A reliable estimate can be made of the amount of the obligation

If these conditions are not met, no provision should be recognised but there should be disclosure of the nature of the obligation and the factors that are relevant in determining the amount and timing of future expenditure.

Is it environmental?
However, before such outlays even fall to be considered for recognition (from an environmental perspective), a view must be taken as to whether the cost properly falls under the heading 'environmental'. One test of this is whether the cost was 'wholly and exclusively' incurred in preventing, reducing or repairing damage to the environment and thus should be labelled as an environmental outlay. A further issue arises when a company moves from end-of-pipe improvements (pollution reduction at the end of the industrial process) to precautionary investment in environmental improvement. End-of-pipe technology is more likely to be readily identifiable as environmental compliance and attributable as such. However, the more a company adopts cleaner production approaches, the more difficult it becomes to identify environmental compliance costs. If environmental management decisions are built into production processes and produce both environmental improvements and cost savings then it is difficult to separate that part of the costs attributable to general management and that part attributable solely to environmental issues.

Measurement

The amount recognised as a provision should be a realistic and prudent estimate of the expenditure required to settle the obligation as at the balance sheet date. The risks and uncertainties that inevitably surround many events and circumstances should be taken into account in reaching the best estimate of the amount of the provision.

Disclosure

Items that are relevant to the evaluation of the economic performance of a company are to be disclosed or incorporated into the balance sheet or profit and loss account. For each class of provision the company should disclose:

- The carrying amount at the beginning and end of the period
- Additional provisions made in the period, including increases in existing provisions
- Amounts used
- Amounts reversed (i.e. unused)
- The change in the discounted amount arising from the passage of time and the effect of any change in the discount rate

Other non-financial matters that should be disclosed include the name of the individual with board-level responsibility for the environment and the internal reporting structure; details of accreditation under external standards, as this facilitates the level of risk management assurance and enhances the wider corporate reputation by demonstrating sustainable and socially responsible business practice. Moreover, since compliance with applicable law must be demonstrated, a disclosure relating to globally applied standards, legal compliance, continuous improvement and long-term strategic objectives may be appropriate.

From a US viewpoint, the Securities and Exchange Commission (SEC) requires disclosure of all material effects of compliance with environmental regulations on required capital, expenditures, earnings and the competitive position of the company. Such disclosure is required in the financial statements under the heading 'Description of business' as well as under the heading 'Legal proceedings'.

DEFINITION OF ENVIRONMENTAL COSTS

For a definition the authors have relied upon the Institute of Chartered Accountants in England and Wales (ICAEW) report *Environmental Issues in Financial Reporting* (October 1996), which followed guidance produced by the Canadian Institute of Chartered Accountants. This interprets environmental costs as being a composite term for the following:

- Environmental measures taken by an entity or on its behalf by others, to prevent, reduce, or repair damage to the environment or to deal with the conservation of resources.
- Environmental losses, i.e. costs incurred by an entity in relation to the environment for which there is no return or benefit, e.g. assets whose costs are irrecoverable due to environmental concerns; damages paid to others for environmental damage; fines or penalties for non-compliance with environmental regulations.

Problems arise when attempting to identify whether a cost or expense relates only to an environmental outlay and can therefore properly be labelled as such or, if it is apparent that it does not, how the cost is then to be treated. Secondly and as an intrinsic part of this identification process, it is necessary to consider whether the cost is to be capitalised in the company's balance sheet or treated as part of its annual expenditure in its Profit and Loss Account. Plainly if it is capital expenditure it is not a 'cost' but an asset, if the latter it is an expense. On the basis that the item is a revenue expenditure, the authors have turned again to the ICAEW for guidance. The argument put forward by the ICAEW is that environmental costs must relate 'wholly and exclusively' not to environmental matters generally but 'to preventing, reducing or repairing damage to the environment', thus it is argued that where the expenditure is incurred to conserve energy or for closure costs, even where the closure takes place for environmental reasons, it is not to be regarded as an environmental cost, since there are other reasons for the expenditure. The writers find this argument untenable if the exercise is merely to label a particular cost or expense, but acceptable if the purpose of the 'labelling' is to identify costs incurred in securing an environmental benefit. It has to be said, however, that even this argument does not sit well with the disallowance of the costs of closure, since it may be that such closure is purely for environmental reasons. Perhaps, therefore, the ICAEW report should be treated as a general statement only, capable of review in appropriate circumstances.

Whatever may be the position, the ICAEW makes it clear that to prevent users of accounts being misled, it is important to ensure that adequate disclosure is made of what the environmental costs actually include or, if relevant, exclude.

As already noted an item of expenditure can have more than one purpose. In those circumstances it may be difficult to distinguish between the element that represents environmental spending and those that do not. For example, if a new plant is built, the capital expenditure is partly in new technology which results inevitably in improved environmental efficiency, but mostly in the new building and equipment which results in greater overall productivity. So the question that arises is, How does the company account for the environmental element? The ICAEW recommends that a judgemental allocation of costs should be made based on the best information available together, if appropriate, with an engineering assessment. Alternatively the 'wholly and exclusively' test should be applied, even where capital expenditure projects are undertaken primarily for environmental reasons.

The ICAEW also has advice to offer on the issue of separate disclosure of environmental costs—there is no need for separate disclosure, unless such costs form an exceptional item. For those looking for environmental expenditure in order to identify the company's position in the environmental hierarchy, this is not helpful advice. However, some of the other key recommendations of the report do assist:

- Environmental costs should be recognised as soon as the company has an obligation to meet them.
- Any environmental costs that are disclosed should be accompanied by a description of the basis adopted, whether from a comprehensive allocation of costs or as a result of the 'wholly and exclusively' approach.
- Environmental costs relating to prior years should not be shown as a prior year adjustment but should instead be charged as a current liability in order to arrive at the profit and loss for that year, with separate disclosure if the amount is material.

- Environmental costs that provide access to future economic benefits, including the continued operation of an asset, should be capitalised.
- Except where a reasonable estimate of an obligation cannot be determined, a provision should be made for all environmental liabilities for which an entity has an obligation, including a constructive obligation.
- An environmental liability should be measured as the estimated amount of future cash flows needed to meet the obligation.
- Environmental liabilities that are contingent on an uncertain future event should be recognised if it is probable that they will arise; if a reasonable estimate of the liability cannot be made, its existence and nature should be disclosed.
- Environmental impairment of an asset should be recognised by reducing the carrying amount so as to reflect its real value.
- Financial statements should include a description of the accounting policies relating to any significant environmental costs and liabilities that are disclosed. There is to be regarded as good practice inclusion of management commentary on any material environmental issues affecting or likely to affect the company.

FRS 12 provides assistance and clarification on some of these issues. It sets out the principles of accounting for provisions, contingent liabilities and contingent assets. Its objective is to ensure that appropriate recognition criteria and measurement bases are applied and that sufficient information is disclosed in the notes to the financial statements to enable users to understand their nature, timing and amount. With limited exceptions, it applies to all financial statements that are intended to give a true and fair view in accounting for provisions, contingent liabilities and contingent assets. Provisions for environmental liabilities should be recognised at the time and to the extent that the company becomes obliged legally or constructively to rectify environmental damage or to perform restorative work on the environment. This effectively confirmed the guidance in the ICAEW report referred to above.

On the international front, the IASC requires the disclosure of contingent losses that are not recognised unless the probability of loss is remote (IAS 10.9), and the United States SEC requires disclosure in the management discussion and analysis of any 'trend, commitment, event or uncertainty' that is 'known' cannot be determined to be 'not reasonably likely to occur' or is reasonably likely to have a material effect on the company's financial condition.

ENVIRONMENTALLY INDUCED COSTS: ASSETS OR EXPENSES?

It is not possible to leave the topic of financial accounting without further consideration of the vexed issue of whether environmental costs (once identified as such) should be treated as capital or revenue items. This is a difficult topic for both auditors and financial analysts and very difficult for the average stakeholder to understand. In principle, under conventional financial accounting, the difference between an expense and an asset is clear. An expense is a cost that has led to a benefit and has now expired, whereas costs that have been incurred that lead to future benefits are classified as assets. In practice it is not easy to determine what the increased or decreased economic benefits of pollution prevention and emission reduction might be. Moreover, and as will be seen, a desire to be tax efficient may not always sit comfortably with a desire to be seen as environmentally proactive.

In its 1993 research report *Environmental costs and liabilities: accounting and financial reporting issues,* the Canadian Institute of Chartered Accountants (CICA) defined environmental measures in the same way as 'environmental costs' referred to above, i.e. those undertaken to:

- Prevent, abate or remediate damage to the environment
- Deal with the conservation of renewable and non-renewable resources

So the first question that arises is: Are the costs capable of capitalisation? Financial statements are prepared in order to report the financial performance of a company and should not be distorted with issues that are not material in financial terms. From a strict economic perspective, capitalisation of costs should be allowed only if those costs contribute to additional future economic benefits.

Perhaps, however, in some special cases, costs of clean-up or pollution prevention may qualify as assets if they are absolutely necessary for the company to stay in business, even though they do not affect expected future cash flows.

And the second question: If the company has a choice, does it wish to capitalise the costs? Revenue expenditure is allowable for tax purposes, that is, it reduces the level of income chargeable to tax. In contrast, capital expenditure is not generally allowable. In English law the principles to be applied in determining whether expenditure is capital or revenue have been established through case law:

- Where expenditure is incurred with a view to bringing into existence an asset or advantage for the enduring[1] benefit of a trade there is a presumption that the expenditure is capital in nature.
- If the payment is a 'one off' payment rather than a recurring one then it is likely to be capital in nature.

However, note that under UK tax law, expenditures such as for obtaining a Pollution Prevention and Control permit for the most polluting processes or for becoming accredited under ISO 14001 or EMAS, are likely to be treated as capital payments and therefore not deductible for tax purposes against income.

The US Financial Accounting Standards Board has a view that costs of environmental contamination should in general be treated as an expense but that capitalisation may be possible in certain circumstances. One thing is plain, without the use of international standards, to which reference is made below, the position is confused and likely to remain so.

THE IASC APPROACH

The International Accounting Standards Committee (IASC) was founded in 1973 with the objective of harmonising the accounting principles which are used by businesses for financial reporting around the world. The committee currently has 153 professional

---

[1] The word 'enduring' is not defined in UK tax legislation but an enduring benefit is generally thought to be one which is expected to last three years or more.

accounting body members spanning 112 countries. As business has become more global, the need for reliable and transparent accounting has increased. Such accounting improves the ability of investors, creditors, governments and others to make informed resource allocation and policy decisions. From an environmental perspective it improves the ability for comparison between companies in different countries in the same or similar industries. A set of International Accounting Standards have been prepared by the IASC and are accepted by many stock exchanges around the world (including the EU) although not those in the US or Canada. In the UK the ICAEW has given its support to the standards which it has said are sufficiently comprehensive for use in financial statements. From a management standpoint the need for multinational companies to prepare accounts on different bases for use in different jurisdictions is highly unsatisfactory because:

- It can cause increased preparation costs.
- Such companies will want to have a uniform system for assessing financial performance in their operations in different countries. They will also want their external reports to be consistent with internal assessments of performance.

It is sensible therefore to look at what the IASC has provided for in relation to the issues discussed above. IAS 16 states that the 'additional cost of future benefits' approach is correct. This means that the disbursement must result in an increase in expected future economic benefits from the asset. IAS 16.14 allows the capitalisation of environmentally related costs for property, plant and equipment if an increase in future economic benefits from other assets is expected and if the costs are recoverable. Capitalisation is possible if the costs are necessary to comply with environmental requirements.

Capital allowances: the UK tax perspective

A capital allowance may be available which will enable a company to obtain a measure of tax relief. The amount of tax relief given will depend on the type of expenditure and the cost of the asset. Presently, under English law, capital allowances are available on expenditure for example, for plant and machinery, industrial buildings and research and development.

The operating and financial review

Standing midway between financial accounting and environmental reporting is the review which generally forms part of the financial accounts. It is worth noting that in the UK, the Advisory Committee on Business and the Environment (ACBE) in its 1996 report pointed out that the Financial Reporting Council strongly recommended that UK listed companies supported operating and financial reviews (OFRs) alongside their annual financial statements, as narrative amplifications of past performance and planned strategic direction. The OFR format as prepared by the Accounting Standards Board explicitly provides for inclusion of environmental information. Thus UK listed companies should ensure that their OFRs include descriptive and quantitative details of the environmental risks they face, the environmental costs they have incurred and the environmental initiatives they have taken. The report suggests that the discussion should be 'linked to the amounts charged, provided for or disclosed in the accounts, and it would thus cover capital and revenue expenditure, liabilities and provisions'. The ACBE also takes the view that the OFR should state whether a formal environmental management system is in place and the extent to which management action has led to changes in the company's environmental performance.

SUMMARY OF ENVIRONMENTAL ACCOUNTING

Management still has considerable discretion in deciding which environmental issues to recognise, how to recognise them, what to disclose and how and where to make the disclosure. While there are a number of initiatives designed to reduce the available choices for management and hence to improve the ability of stakeholders to make more informed decisions and to become more aware of potential environmental risks, none of these has been universally accepted and thus no level playing field yet exists (Table 4.1).

Table 4.1 *A chronology of environmental accounting and reporting*[a]

1991	ACCA introduced an industry environmental reporting award
1994	ACCA award was extended to companies within the EU
1995	EU published *Accounting Advisory Forum report, Environmental Issues in Financial Reporting*
1995	Auditing Practices Board introduced SAS120
1995	US financial reporting standards cause pressure on UK listed companies
1996	ASB discussion paper on environmental provisions
1997	ACBE published *Environmental Reporting and the Financial Sector: an approach to good practice*
1997	ASB Financial Reporting exposure draft: *Provisions and contingencies* (FRED 14) and *Impairment of fixed assets* (FRED 15)
1998	Financial Reporting Standard FRS 12: *Provisions, contingent liabilities and contingent assets*
2000	GRI published *Sustainablility Reporting Guidelines*

[a] ACCA = Association of Chartered Certified Accountants, ASB = Accounting Standards Board, ACBE = Advisory Committee on Business and the Environment, GRI = Global Reporting Initiative

ENVIRONMENTAL REPORTING

According to ISAR (Intergovernmental Working Group of Experts on International Standards of Accounting and Reporting of the United Nations), 'environmental reporting' is the term

> now commonly used to describe the disclosure by an entity of environmentally related data, verified (audited) or not, regarding environmental risks, environmental impacts, policies, strategies, targets, costs, liabilities, or environmental performance.

Thus it forms part of the toolbox enabling stakeholders and others to form their view of the environmental worth of a company. An environmental report can be:

- Contained within the annual report and accounts
- A stand-alone corporate environmental performance report
- A report limited to the environmental issues relating to a particular site in which case it may be the environmental statement produced by every company accredited under EMAS
- Produced in some other form, e.g. a staff newsletter

The Environmental Task Force of the European Federation of Accountants defines the objective of external environmental reporting in a similar way:

> the provision of information about the environmental impact and operational performance of an entity that is useful to relevant stakeholders in assessing their relationship with the reporting entity.

These definitions are of course similar to the definition of the use of financial accounting proposed earlier: to assist the company and its stakeholders and the wider public to ascertain the financial position, performance and changes in financial position of a company, whether or not for the purpose of making economic decisions with respect to it.

The benefits of environmental reporting vary from company to company. However, it is possible to identify several issues that may be a common thread:

- The extent to which the environmental management system implements the environmental policy and is an integral part of its overall corporate plan and business operations.
- That management is committed to environmental issues (as demonstrated in the point above) serves to enhance employee or workforce morale, by top-down leadership.
- Publishing performance standards drives continuous improvement (which is, in any event, probably required by the environmental management system).
- Establishes environmental issues as a key policy and strategy element of the company's focus.
- Enables companies to reassure investors and lenders as to environmental risk.

Moreover, the environmental report demonstrates corporate environmental engagement and this demonstration may:

- Enable good environmental performers to differentiate themselves from other companies in their peer group
- Allow them to 'punch above their weight'
- Minimise risk of regulatory intervention

- Create local community opportunities
- Provide improved access to supply chain (including public procurement opportunities)
- Provide quality public relations and profiling opportunities

Finally, the audit and report culture once instilled in a company will make the company more receptive to new developments, e.g. social and ethical reporting.

DIFFERENT APPROACHES TO ENVIRONMENTAL REPORTING

Different methodological approaches to environmental reporting have evolved, mainly because of local, cultural or regulatory differences in compliance-based reporting. Here are the principal approaches.

Compliance reporting

Reporting the level of compliance with external regulations and consent limits is a common feature of the environmental reports of heavily regulated utilities (e.g. water, electricity).

Toxic release inventory based reporting

Many US companies are required by law to publish lists (detailed in physical quantities) of emissions of specific toxic substances.

Impact-based performance reporting

Most private sector companies that are not subject to specific consent requirements, identify their key environmental impacts and base their reporting around target setting and performance (over time) in achieving those targets.

The eco-balance approach

Some companies (including many from Germany) construct a formal 'eco-balance' (resource input versus product and non-product output) from which they then derive performance indicators.

The environmental burden approach

The UK chemicals manufacturer ICI has developed an externally focused reporting approach which quantifies the company's impact on a number of environmental quality measures.

Greenhouse gas indicator

Converting energy use from all sources into a measure of carbon dioxide (CO_2) emissions (and other greenhouse gases) which can be expressed by say unit of turnover. This indicator was developed by UNEP in conjunction with National Provident Institution and Imperial College London.

Triple bottom line/sustainability reporting

Sustainability reporting involves combining environmental reporting with the reporting of financial and social performance measures. The form of the environmental report may, to some extent, be determined by its audience (Table 4.2). Stakeholders cover a multiplicity of different groups each with a different agenda. If structured for a financial audience then the key messages will be strategic; if for a wider community then soft issues, such as enhancement of the environment through projects and grants, may be to the fore. Whichever it may be, it must be factually accurate. The operating and financial review referred to earlier leads naturally to the need for information in the environmental report to be compatible with that in the OFR and in the accounts, and there should be adequate cross-references between them.

Table 4.2 *Table of guidelines for environmental reporting*[a]

Organisation	Guideline	Place of origin
ACBE	Environmental reporting and the financial sector: an approach to good practice	UK
ACCA	Environment and energy reporting	UK
CBI	Introducing environmental reporting	UK
CEFIC	Responsible care, health, safety, and environmental reporting guidelines	Europe
CERES	Formats for an environmental report	US
CICA	Reporting on environmental performance	Canada
CMA	Management accounting guidelines	Canada
[b]	Coming clean 1993 (the first guidance)	International
DETR	Environmental reporting: getting started[c]	UK
DIN	DIN 33922	Germany
FEEM	Guidelines for preparation of company environmental reports	Italy
GEMI	Environmental reporting: tools and publications	US
INEM	Environmental reports	Germany
NSNE[d]	Guide to mandatory environmental reporting in the Netherlands	Netherlands
NSW EPA	Corporate environmental reporting	Australia
PERI	Guidelines	Cross-border

[a] ACBE = Advisory Committee on Business and the Environment, CEFIC = European Chemical Industry Council, CERES = Coalition for Environmentally Responsible Economies (a pressure group and a group of environmentally forward thinking companies), CMA = Society of Management Accountants of Canada, DETR = Department of the Environment Transport and the Regions, DIN = German standardisation body, FEEM = Forum on Environmental Reporting, GEMI = Global Environmental Management Initiative, INER = International Network for Environmental Reporting, NCW = Dutch employers organisation, NSNE = Netherlands Society for Nature and Environment, NSW EPA = New South Wales Environmental Protection Agency, PERI = Public Environmental Reporting Initiative, founded 1992
[b] Produced by IISD, Deloitte Touche Tohmatsu, SustainAbility
[c] A series of booklets on different topics
[d] With VNO-NCW

GRI SUSTAINABILITY REPORTING GUIDELINES

The Global Reporting Initiative (GRI) was established in 1997 with the mission of developing globally applicable guidelines for reporting on economic, social and environmental performance. It was convened by the Coalition for Environmentally Responsible Economies in partnership with UNEP. The authors have chosen to focus on the work of the GRI, as the progress of the exposure draft first issued in 1999 is well documented and it has been well supported by companies from around the world.

Twenty-one pilot test companies, numerous other companies and non-corporate stakeholders commented on the draft guidelines during a pilot-test period during 1999 and 2000, and revised guidelines were issued in June 2000. Although the suggested form of report goes further than the mere reporting of environmental issues, to the more complex sustainability issues, there is little doubt that leading-edge companies are looking closely at sustainability reporting rather than confining their efforts to the narrower issues of the environment.

Much of what follows is based on the guidelines and the authors are grateful to the GRI Interim Secretariat for permission to use this material. The guidelines may be freely downloaded from www.globalreporting.org.

Incremental adoption of the GRI reporting format

The GRI Sustainability Reporting Guidelines on Economic, Environmental and Social Performance, to give their full title, allow for companies wishing to progress incrementally towards a complete GRI report using some of the individual elements initially, provided there is full disclosure of such incremental adoption as follows:

- A statement that the GRI guidelines have been used and the extent of that use
- The reasons for incremental adoption, e.g. expense, availability of information, stakeholder needs
- Their intentions regarding the future production of a complete GRI report

The elements of a GRI report

The guidelines break down into principles which are to be followed and this should give consistency to all reports which follow the guidelines, thus allowing the reader to compare one report with another.

The reporting scope principle

This first principle ensures that the company makes clear the scope of its reporting activities and if it does not cover all economic, social and environmental matters, then it sets out which issues are covered.

The reporting period principle

Under this principle, the company should ensure as far as possible that reportable impacts, events and activities are included in the correct reporting period and not held up for any reason. In practice this should mean that a fugitive emission from a plant which causes contamination should be reported in the report cycle in which it occurs, not when the contamination is identified. Moreover, because management should be concerned to integrate economic, environmental and social issues into overall corporate strategy, over time the systems should become aligned with conventional systems for financial management and control.

The going-concern principle

This principle assumes that the published data will reflect the assumption that the reporting company is likely to remain in business for the foreseeable future. In order to meet the assumption from a financial standpoint, the company is generally expected to be financially viable. Although in financial reporting terms this is rarely more than 18 months after balance sheet date, GRI asks for a broader interpretation of that narrow financial principle. So, for example, it suggests the company should take into account in the appropriate section of the GRI report, any 'going concern' qualifications contained in the financial audit report; any qualifications regarding the company's ability to fund any necessary remediation; the extent to which significant internal and external operational, financial, compliance and other risks are identified and assessed on an ongoing basis (e.g. those related to environmental or reputational issues); the likely impact of prospective legislation (e.g. product or environmental); management's assessment of the consequences (including economic and social consequences) of moving towards modes of production and or service delivery compatible with sustainability.

The conservatism principle
The company must claim credit only for those achievements that can be directly attributed to it. Moreover, it must be cautious in reporting expected future outcomes of current programmes. The GRI encourages life cycle approaches and reporting of upstream and downstream effects of operations and activities. The report should, however, be balanced, containing both positive and negative effects of the company's operations.

The materiality principle
The application of the materiality concept to economic, environmental and social reporting is more complex than in financial reporting. There is no quantative basis for GRI reporting as there is for financial reporting. Thus the company must decide what is material based on the nature or circumstances of an event and whether therefore it is necessary to report upon it. So in environmental terms, the carrying capacity of the receiving media, say the watershed, will be just one of several factors in the materiality of the release of one tonne or even one kilogram of waste.

Qualitative characteristics
The GRI set out various qualitative characteristics for the report, which range from relevance on the one hand, through clarity, to comparability on the other hand. The guidelines also require formal disclosure of all significant reporting and measurement policies, and most importantly, set out the headings for report content; these are considered in detail in the following section.

The contents of the GRI report

CEO statement
The contents are not prescriptive but GRI recommends inclusion of the following elements: highlights of report content and commitment to targets; declaration of commitment to economic, social

and environmental goals by the company management; acknowledgement of successes and failures; performance against benchmarks, previous years' performance targets and industry sector norms; and major challenges for the company and its business sector in integrating responsibilities for financial performance with those for economic environmental and social performance along with the implications of this on future business strategy.

Profile of reporting company

The report must provide an overview of the reporting company and the scope of the report. This is to give readers a context for understanding and evaluating the information contained in the report and should provide company contacts. It is not appropriate to set out at length the contents of this section. Suffice it to say that it must encompass such matters as the major products and/or services; the countries of operation; the nature of markets served; the scale of activities (e.g. number of employees); breakdown of sales or revenues by country or region, where their sales account for more than 5% of total revenues, as well as by major products; the coverage of the report, and if not complete, the projected timescale for complete coverage; reporting period and date of the most recent previous report (if any); significant changes that have occurred in the accounting period; public accessibility of information and details of how to obtain it.

Executive summary and key indicators

The executive summary is a key component of the report. While there is no guarantee that readers will ever read the whole of a document, most will read the executive summary and GRI therefore requires that it should contain a summary of important information, presented in such a style that is easily assimilated. It must contain as a minimum:

- The specified generally applicable environmental performance indicators[2]
- Selected company-specific environmental performance indicators
- Selected economic performance indicators
- Selected integrated performance indicators

[2] These general indicators are specified in the guidelines and if for any reason the company does not report on them, it must explain why.

- Historical trends for at least the last two reporting periods and a target period

Vision and strategy

This section should include the management of challenges associated with economic, environmental and social performance. (Economic performance should include financial performance but it should contain other economic items too.) This may include a discussion of how economic, environmental and social goals and values intersect and are balanced in the company, and how such linkages and balancing shape the company's decision-making processes. The GRI indicates that the company should use maximum creativity and flexibility in this section, consistent presumably with the overriding principle of conservatism.

Policies, organisation and management systems

This section should include, among other things, mission and values statements, whether the precautionary principle is addressed by reference to the company's policies, and the organisational structure and responsibilities in the company. It should also include details of the management systems, including employee orientation and awareness, environmental accounting auditing practices, approaches to measuring and improving management quality, programmes and procedures for outsourcing, supplier chain selection criteria, and programmes for decisions regarding location of operations. The company should also deal with the basis for definition and selection of major stakeholders and any approaches to them.

Performance

This section should contain an overview, which in fact must contain very detailed information by reference to indicators, broken down over all the relevant sectors. The overview should be divided into four parts:

- Environmental performance
- Economic performance
- Social performance
- Integrated performance

It is the information in this section relating to performance indicators, and the feedback GRI derives from the users of the guidance, that will enable GRI to provide enhanced versions of the guidance over time. Some examples of indicators are energy, materials use, water use, emissions, profits, investments and suppliers.

It is clear that those companies which choose to frame their sustainability reports based on the GRI guidelines are aspiring to provide complete data, enabling stakeholders properly to evaluate not only the activities of the company but also the statements made by management. GRI also makes it plain that they monitor initiatives taken by other organisations, non-governmental organisations (NGOs) and professional bodies, with a view in the future to incorporating and/or accommodating portions of complementary initiatives, while remaining true to its overarching principles.

INDEPENDENT REVIEW

Whatever the format of the report, whether it follows the GRI guidelines or some other format, its credibility, quality and usefulness will be enhanced through independent verification. Different forms of review may be appropriate for different parts of the material presented. Environmental liabilities and costs will be reported in the accounts, as will social and economic information if the report extends to sustainability issues, and these financial matters will be subject to financial audit. Physical information, whether in the OFR or in the environmental or sustainability report, may be externally scrutinised. An environmental report may be 'audited' by the external EMS verifiers. Their skills differ, and in order to bring greatest credibility to the report, it might be prudent to use one of the bigger accountancy firms that can carry out environmental and sustainability auditing.

If for any reason the company does not elect for independent verification, perhaps because it needs time to assess its needs or readiness for independent review, then other options might be a statement in the report that it has been subject to internal auditing of systems and procedures, or a directors' responsibility statement.

CONCLUSION

The company that chooses to account and report environmentally is, to an extent, laying itself on the line, inviting criticism (and praise) for its activities and helping in the long process of building up a bank of information as to how companies perform under certain circumstances and in certain fields. From the perspective of the stakeholder, some conclusions can be drawn from the form and content of the environmental report. But beyond everything, the stakeholder wishes to be able to identify the strong performer. Although this topic is dealt with in detail elsewhere in the book, here are some general points:

- The company that chooses one of the well-respected methodologies for the preparation of environmental accounts, may have less to hide.
- The company that provides a directors' responsibility statement which makes it evident that there is clear board approval for the report, is plainly serious about its perceived reporting obligations.
- The company that has an accredited environmental management system probably takes its environmental responsibilities in earnest.
- The company that is prepared to give the public easy access to environmental information may be on top of its sensitive issues.
- The company that uses one of the well-respected methodologies for environmental reporting, and even better, is committed to sustainability reporting, is likely to be a leading-edge company.

CHAPTER 5

Socially Responsible Investing

A SHORT HISTORY OF ETHICAL INVESTMENT

The history of ethical investment is a venerable one.[1] Not a child of the twentieth century, as might have been expected, but rooted in religious principles. For example the Friends Provident, which was founded in 1832 to provide life assurance for the Society of Friends, more often called the Quakers. They rapidly built up investment funds but never invested in companies with business activities which involved slavery. In the early 1900s the Methodist Church wished to start investing in the stock market but refused to invest in companies with alcohol, tobacco or gambling as part of their business.

In 1971 the United States Pax World Fund was set up in response to the demand for investments which did not benefit the Vietnam War, thus pre-dating the launch of ethical unit trusts in the UK by more than a decade. And so it continued; in protest against the effects of apartheid in South Africa, some shareholders lobbied their companies not to do business there. This early form of shareholder coercion was partly responsible for the creation of the modern approach to ethical investment. At the edge of mainstream investment, ethical

---

[1] Ethical investment is defined by UKSIF as the purchase of stocks and shares which have been selected by combining ethical screening with conventional financial criteria. Socially responsible investment is defined by UKSIF as transactions which invest money (taking account of the investors' values and objectives) in such a way that it can be realised by repayment or trading with or without an additional financial return.

investment funds were initially seen as being for those with an advanced social conscience or perhaps eccentrics.

In the 1980s ethical investment came into its own. For all the reasons propounded in Chapter 1 – damage to the environment, the recognition that the few could not continue depleting the Earth's resources at the expense of the many, the increasing weight of environmental legislation, the acknowledgement of the need for more sustainable development, and the need to reduce pollution emissions – many considered it appropriate to signal a change from conventional investing policies to investments in companies with a positive ethical edge.

Ethical investment enthusiasts wanting a common source of research on company activities set up the Ethical Investment Research Service in 1983. Then, the following year, Friends Provident founded their Stewardship fund, which in February 2001 had over £1 billion under ethical management, against an original anticipated market of £2 million. Jupiter Asset Management launched an authorised 'green' unit trust in 1988 (the Ecology Fund) which invests in companies worldwide that are responding positively to and profiting from the challenge of environmental sustainability and are making positive commitment to social well-being.

The Ecology Fund aimed to encourage the adoption of higher environmental and social standards and offered investors, for the first time, the opportunity to invest in companies likely to benefit from the transition to a sustainable future. Meanwhile, other vehicles for socially responsible investment were starting. Mercury Provident (now Triodos Bank) was set up as a bank in 1974 to lend to projects with a social benefit. Seven years later the Ecology Building Society began financing the purchase of properties with an ecological payback. The trade-union-backed Unity Trust Bank arrived in 1984, and ethical banking received an important boost in 1992 when the Co-operative Bank introduced its highly successful ethical policy. Specialist social finance organisations such as Industrial Common Ownership Finance began to seek 'socially directed investments', offering a high social return with zero or low interest.

But before that, at the beginning of the 1990s, Pensions & Investment Research Consultants Limited (PIRC) was founded. Its objectives were, although not initially, to give advice on corporate governance, and to provide a socially responsible investment service to provide all the information and support institutional investors need to pursue practical and effective socially responsible investment policies. The service is based on the key stakeholder relationships at a local and international level. PIRC monitors five areas:

- *Environment*: corporate policies, the quality of reporting, management systems, independent verification
- *Employment*: training programmes, consultation procedures, representative structures, participation, equal opportunities
- *Human rights*: overseas labour standards, involvement with repressive regimes, arms industry
- *Community policy*: charitable and political donations
- *Corporate governance*: shareholder rights, best practice compliance, board structures, remuneration, investor relations

Other such organisations began to appear, all offering variations on the common theme of identification of socially responsible companies, but the next development of note was the recognition of the need for asset managers specialising in socially responsible investments.

Sustainable Asset Management (SAM) was established in 1995 as an independent asset management company headquartered in Zurich, Switzerland. SAM was early in the field of asset managers to specialise in the field of sustainability-driven investments. SAM's customers include major European banks, global insurance companies, large pension funds and private clients. SAM manages institutional and private mandates in line with sustainability criteria and offers sustainability-driven investment vehicles such as the Sustainable Performance Group and various mutual funds. It was in 1999 that SAM, together with Dow Jones & Company, launched the world's first index to track the performance of sustainability-driven companies worldwide.

When making an initial judgement on the suitability of potential investment opportunities, ethical investment funds rely on simple screening techniques. Screening may be defined as 'the inclusion or exclusion of corporate securities in investment portfolios based on social or environmental criteria' (Social Investment Forum definition). The original ethical or green funds concentrated on negative screening principles. That is, investment could not take place in companies with interests in businesses involving arms manufacture, alcohol, tobacco, gambling and treasury securities.[2] But it soon came to be seen that there was a better way to select companies and that was by using positive screening methods. It is not difficult to anticipate the criteria for positive screening:

- Respectable employee relations
- Strong record of community involvement
- Excellent environmental impact policies
- Respect for human rights around the world
- Safe and useful products[3]

It is also easy to see that negative screening can be broadened out to encompass not just types of business but any business whose performance in the key areas mentioned above is inadequate.

In the UK, the Pensions Act 1995 required each pension fund to prepare a Statement of Investment Principles (SIP) setting out its investment policies. The act was amended by regulations in 1999 so that, from July 2000, fund trustees were required to expand the issues covered in SIPs to state 'the extent (if at all) to which social environmental or ethical considerations are taken into account in the selection retention and realisation of investments' (SI 1999 1849). And thus socially responsible investing came to the forefront of public awareness (at least that part of the public with an interest in its retirement funds). The regulations undoubtedly open up new ways for corporate policies and practices to be challenged by environmental groups as well as the financial community. The regulations also required trustees to state their policy on the exercise of their voting rights.

It is worth quoting Stephen Timms, the UK pensions minister at the time the regulation was published. Speaking at a Forum for the Future seminar in London in 1999, he said:

> There is undoubtedly a significant groundswell of public interest in socially responsible investment. Ordinary people want to

---

[2] Because the treasury, whether in the UK, the US or elsewhere in the world, invests some of its funds in making war not peace.

[3] Social Investment Forum screening techniques.

know what is being done with the money invested on their behalf.

I believe that this Regulation will stimulate the debate on socially responsible investment further and increase transparency in investment planning.

SIPs must cover the types of investment, the balance between investments, risk, return and realisation and now the policy on socially responsible investment. However, the regulations do not oblige fund trustees to accept socially responsible investments and they may say that such do not influence their decisions. The regulation does not apply solely to private pension funds, it also applies to local authority pension funds which are regulated by DEFRA. The effect of this is to pitch considerable sums into socially responsible investments and to encourage the local authorities to drive forward the search for social responsibility. Other examples of pension fund trustees early into consideration of socially responsible investment objectives are BT, with assets of about £29 billion, and the Universities Superannuation Scheme, with assets of about £20 billion.

As there has been a push towards socially responsible investment, so there has been government pressure for increased environmental reporting. DEFRA minister Michael Meacher threatened to name and shame those FTSE companies that did not provide an environmental report, and in early 2001 there were many of them. The perception in some companies is that environmental reports are an unnecessary expense However, the perception of the need for environmental accounting and reporting may change both as a result of the regulations and because of the Department of Trade and Industry (DTI) report referred to below.

If companies environmental reports were prepared in a way that suited the financial community, such reports would no doubt gain in popularity, at least among fund managers, if not at board level. As it is, they tend to be glossy brochures designed for local communities, non-governmental organisations (NGOs) and pressure groups. However, the DTI in its last company law review (2000) looked at the issues surrounding environmental reporting. Although it stopped

111

short of making such reports mandatory, it did recommend that companies should report annually on their environmental performance and liabilities. The review also indicated that directors' duties should be extended to cover environmental and social issues, although these are to remain subordinate to promotion of shareholder value.

But it should not be thought that only a minority of the British investing public are interested in socially responsible investing. An increasing number of consumers have ethical and social concerns. Green and ethical consumers form a major group within the population, as a relatively recent MORI poll has indicated. In August 2000 Friends Ivory and Sime plc and NOP reported that 74% of occupational pension scheme members (based on a survey of 1,000) thought it important that their pension fund tried to use its influence to encourage socially responsible behaviour by companies.

Interestingly, where a company had a poor environmental or ethical record, 72% thought their pension fund should use its influence to encourage change, and only 21% preferred their fund to avoid investment in such company. Moreover, according to the UK Social Investment Forum (UKSIF), the increase in ethical consumers is also evidenced by the growth in funds invested ethically, which since 1989 has outstripped all unit and investment trusts in every year except one. In the two years to January 1999, the total funds managed by ethical unit and investment trusts has almost doubled from £1.1 billion to £2.1 billion according to the Ethical Investment Research Service (EIRIS). And the figure is £2.6 billion according to UKSIF. As of August 2001 EIRIS reports the figure to be almost £4 billion.

Next for discussion in the chronological history of ethical investment is the Financial Services Authority (FSA), which regulates UK financial services. The FSA is empowered by the Financial Services and Markets Act 2000. However, there is a view that this Act may not be sufficiently robust from a socially responsible investment standpoint. UKSIF, for example, raised three areas of concern relating to the regulator's powers under the Act: the lack of any mention of the regulator's role in contributing to sustainable development; the need to ensure consumers are educated about the social and environmental impact of their investments; and the need to protect the green and ethical consumer. It may be that further legislation is required to ensure that green and ethical consumers' ethical, social and environmental concerns are taken into account in relation to different kinds of financial regulated activities. Ethical, social and environmental concerns, in this connection, include consideration of the range and nature of impacts of investment and finance on individuals, society and the environment. But it is early days, and as time passes, the position will no doubt become clearer.

And finally, if further evidence were required to demonstrate that the evolution of socially responsible investing is ongoing, then it is only necessary to look at *Buried Treasure: the business case for corporate sustainability*, a report commissioned by the United Nations Environment Programme (UNEP) from SustainAbility.[4] This report was presented at the UNEP high-level meeting in Nairobi in February 2001. On page 98, we referred to triple bottom line accounting, the goal of many leading-edge companies. The triple bottom line could be described as the original three pillars of sustainable development – social, environmental and economic. Thus, over time, although the name has changed, the goal has not.

Buried Treasure claims that corporate triple bottom line programmes, (the three pillars) do show a real and positive pay-off. Based on international research, its findings indicate that a strategic focus on sustainable development is significantly and positively aligned with mainstream business success. SustainAbility mapped ten dimensions of corporate sustainable development against ten indicators of business success covering financial and intangible assets. It found that in the overwhelming majority of instances there was a 'weak' to 'moderate' positive link between the management of sustainable development and business performance and in some cases a very strong correlation between financial competence and social responsibility (Tables 5.1 and 5.2).

The matrix demonstrates that not only is there a relationship between sustainable development performance and enhanced corporate reputation and brand value, but that the relationship is inverse: 'Poor sustainable development performance – across one or more

---

[4] SustainAbility, a strategic management consultancy and think-tank founded in 1987, is dedicated to promoting the business case for sustainable development. It has three main areas of operation: foresight, agenda setting and change management.

Table 5.1 *Measurements of business success*[a]

	Financial performance
1	Shareholder value
2	Revenue
3	Operational efficiency
4	Access to capital
	Financial drivers
5	Customer attraction
6	Brand value and reputation
7	Human and intellectual capital
8	Risk profile
9	Innovation
10	Licence to operate

[a] Source: Sustainability: Buried Treasure: uncovering the business case for corporate sustainability

dimensions – can be more strongly associated with damage to brand value and reputation than superior sustainable development performance can be related to enhancement.' The report also seeks to show that there are significant links to other business success dimensions, such as shareholder value, operational efficiency, human and intellectual capital, and risk profile.

And so the question is (and this, determines the future of socially responsible investment), If green products match conventional products on quality (and price), will an environmentally sound product boost sales? Will it also stimulate innovation and bring efficiencies (e.g. through waste reduction) using approaches such as green design, or design for the environment as it is sometimes called?

It is said, and indeed it is demonstrated in this book, that there are gains to be made for industry and for the environment if companies pursue environmentally sound policies. The research carried out by SustainAbility suggests there is hard evidence pointing to a link between respecting the environment and enhanced profitability. At a time when there appears to be a downturn in the world economy, it is those companies which can find a competitive edge that will the more easily survive. If that edge proves to be a demonstration of a

Table 5.2 *Dimensions of corporate sustainable development performance[a]*

Governance
1 Ethics, values and principles
2 Accountability and transparency

General
3 Triple bottom line commitment

Environment
4 Environment process focus
5 Environment product focus

Socio-economic
6 Socio-economic development
7 Human rights
8 Workplace conditions

Stakeholder engagement
9 Emerging business partners
10 Engaging non-business partners

---

[a] Source: Sustainability: Buried Treasure: uncovering the business case for corporate sustainability

causal connection between environment and profit, then this will be to the significant benefit of the environment; without it, when funds are scarce, companies are unlikely to subscribe to sustainable development unless there is evidence of an economic reason to do so.

In the context of this short history of socially responsible investment, it is plain that sustainable development, environmental issues and community issues now all form part of what is required when judging an acceptable investment (Tables 5.1 and 5.2).

RESEARCH METHODOLOGY

Having established the background to socially responsible investment, a number of questions arise:

- Is this fund a socially responsible investment in more than name?
- Are there any benchmarks which could be adopted to demonstrate that companies within a socially responsible investment fund are environmentally well managed?
- Does 'green' really have a beneficial effect on the bottom line?

Or put another way, How does a fund decide upon the criteria to be used in deciding whether an investment is acceptable (including providing a respectable return for investors)? Plainly criteria cannot be set in stone and plainly each fund will receive different advice from its advice committee. However, there is certain generic information which should always be sought (e.g. relating to environmental management systems) and which forms part of the decision process. Moreover, as has been seen, traditional ethical investment used to focus on negative screening techniques followed by the application of usual financial criteria to a limited number of potential investees. When the market was small and expertise great, this may have been adequate but perhaps it is no longer.

Smaller pension funds have a real problem. They need to comply with the 1999 Regulations but they do not have the in-house expertise. Some are instructing investment management companies to provide them with the necessary information on which to make their decisions, but they too may lack in-house experience. Accordingly, they look to the open market where such organisations as Innovest can provide underlying data, or they can simply rely on information obtained from such sources as the Dow Jones Sustainability Group Index. And thus can be seen the rapid development of a new industry – companies that build up environmental profiles of organisations based on questionnaires, publicly available information and interviews.

These schemes benchmark companies against one another to allow comparisons and to identify the best and the worst performers. However, since there is no benchmarking standard, results may not be predictable and since some rating agencies focus on management and some on performance, the playing field is anything but level. Add to this the fact that most agencies rely on self-assessment questionnaires, and it is plain that the margin for error is great. Environmental rating is in its infancy and techniques are still developing. It is undoubtedly needed, and where there is a need it will in time be filled. Until then one solution is to rely on a fund with a well-honed knowledge of the issues.

THE MORLEY APPROACH

Some fund managers with considerable experience and track record, for example Morley Fund Management Ltd advising Norwich Union Sustainable Future funds, take a more radical approach to defining companies fit for a socially responsible investment fund.

Morley consider that an analysis of acceptable sustainable development practices is the foundation for their work. Their premise is that there must be a shift by world economies from environmentally and socially unsustainable growth to sustainable growth and that this will be one of the key forces in the twenty-first century. Thus, in their view, the companies most likely to grow consistently over the next few decades will be those promoting or benefiting from sustainable economic development. A company that is prepared for and that may benefit from the environmental and social challenges facing its business is likely to be well managed and better able to take advantage of the opportunities arising from sustainable development. In their opinion, companies making a direct link between sustainable development and long-term returns and companies providing win-win solutions to environmental and social problems are all likely to do well.

Much of the skill in company profiling is determining the criteria by which to measure the company. The following are suggested by Morley:

- Identify specific environmental and social opportunities and risks
- Judge the suitability of the company for the particular fund
- Highlight areas suitable and pertinent for positive engagement

Morley then grade the company using business sustainability and management vision and strategy as their broad guidelines. A grading system is used for determining the business sustainability (Table 5.3).

Table 5.3 *Grading business sustainability: the Morley system*

Grading	Business sustainablility
A	Core business is sustainable 'solution'; helps overcome some of the key hurdles to sustainable development
B	Business has low impacts and some benefits; may contribute to enabling a more sustainable future
C	Business broadly neutral to sustainability
D	Business creates sustainablility problems (perhaps partly offset by some benefits) but scope to address through strategic change
E	Business is fundamentally in conflict with sustainable development

Here are some examples of core businesses that have been categorised as E:

- Manufacture of cigarettes and other tobacco products
- Ownership, management or construction of nuclear power stations
- Manufacture or marketing of armaments, including weapons, weapon platforms and munitions
- Any company whose principal business involves gambling
- Any company deriving a significant proportion of its turnover from the manufacture and sale of alcohol
- Management vision and opportunities

Table 5.4 shows the grading system for determining the management vision and strategy element. Morley have designed an appraisal matrix (Table 5.5); boxes with a heavy tint are appropriate for the Norwich Union Sustainable Future funds.

Companies within the approved segment in the appraisal matrix are not automatically included in the Norwich Union Sustainable Future funds. They must also meet the rigorous financial criteria dictated by the fund manager. Thus, every company must satisfy three criteria – social, environmental and financial – and if this has a familiar ring, it is hardly surprising.

Finally the Morley Fund Management investment approach requires engagement with the companies in the Norwich Union Sustainable Future funds portfolio. It recognises that engagement is

Table 5.4 *Grading management: the Morley system*

Grading	Description
1 = excellent	Management has a clear vision of sustainable development and is actively working to achieve it. A comprehensive range of high-quality policies, programmes and reporting exist throughout the company
2 = good	Company's understanding and vision of sustainability is incomplete or lacks credibility because it is unwilling to make fundamental changes. It has adopted good policies and best practice in most areas
3 = average	Company's vision omits key social or environmental responsibilities. Reasonable number of policies and programmes, but they are incomplete or poorly implemented
4 = fair	No real vision exists, and social or environmental responsibilities are barely recognised. Company has a few policies but these are not effectively implemented. Awareness of risks is low and it lacks the ability to manage them
5 = poor	Has negligible social or environmental policies. It is unaware of significant social or environmental risks and/or lacks ability to manage them. Company is unreceptive to the concept of corporate social responsibility

an integral and important element of their work and that no company is 'perfect'. Many have significant room for improvement in certain areas, and Morley is therefore prepared to use its position as an actual or potential shareholder to encourage companies to improve their social and environmental performance. Like Friends Provident, Morley have set up an advisory committee that includes three highly respected independent social and environmental experts.

However, not all fund managers have the breadth of experience evidenced by Morley and not all investors know how to separate the good environmental managers from the inadequate. Environmental reports do not, as indicated, necessarily assist in getting to the right information, and while benchmarking is becoming popular, there are few standardised metrics and companies rarely report environmental issues using the same benchmarks, making comparison all but impossible.

Table 5.5 *Management vision and opportunities: the Morley appraisal matrix*

	1	2	3	4	5
A					X
B					X
C				X	X
D	X	X	X	X	X
E	X	X	X	X	X

THE FRIENDS PROVIDENT SYSTEM

Friends Provident defines ethical investment as 'supporting companies which make a positive contribution to society and encouraging
others to cease harmful practices'. This, however, is wider than the
traditional definition of ethical investment and tends much more
towards the broader intentions of socially responsible investment.
Friends Provident wishes companies in its investment portfolio to

120

adopt 'best practice' on social ethical and environmental issues. It focuses on four key themes:

- Environmental management
- Climate change
- Human rights
- Labour standards

Its Ethics Unit advises the Committee of Reference on what position to take on a variety of issues. According to present advice, the following are some activities that Friends Provident consider make a positive contribution to society:

- Supplying the basic necessities of life
- Providing high-quality products and services which are of long-term benefit to the community
- Conservation of energy or natural resources
- Environmental improvements and pollution control
- Good relations with customers and suppliers
- Good employment practices, training and education
- Strong community involvement
- A good equal opportunities record
- Openness about company activities

Here are some activities which in their view harm the world or its inhabitants and thus provide a negative screen:

- Environmental damage and pollution
- Unnecessary exploitation of animals
- Trade with or operations in oppressive regimes
- Exploitation of Third World countries
- Manufacture and sale of weapons
- Nuclear power
- Tobacco or alcohol production
- Gambling
- Pornography
- Offensive or misleading advertising

Friends Provident emphasises, however, that investments continue to be made solely on a financial basis.

THE DOW JONES SUSTAINABLILITY GROUP INDEX

The Dow Jones Sustainablility Group Index was founded in September 1999 by Dow Jones and Sustainable Asset Management, who not only recognised a growing trend in socially responsible investing but also realised there was a gap in the market for providing information. The theory was to create a global index screening companies according to their sustainablility, assessed according to certain criteria devised by the partnership, including financial quantification of each company's sustainability and its management of sustainablility opportunities, risks and costs. Now, sustainablility as a concept may not be difficult to define (although it is notoriously difficult to pursue in practice) and the intention of the index is to provide a benchmark for sustainable performance, against which companies may measure their progress. Its use can be extended beyond a sustainability fund to any type of fund (e.g. an environmental fund or a socially responsible fund) that wishes to be benchmarked against sustainability criteria.

The assessment criteria employed by the Dow Jones Sustainability Group Index do not, in truth, appear greatly different to the sifting processes used by funds which encompass socially responsible or ethical companies, even though the headline reference is to 'sustainablility'. Dow Jones itself says, 'Sustainability companies not only manage the standard economic factors affecting their businesses but the environmental and social factors as well. There is mounting evidence that their financial performance is superior to that of companies that do not adequately correctly and optimally manage these important factors.' The next chapter investigates this 'mounting' evidence by reference to the reports and accounts of a variety of companies.

THE FTSE4GOOD INDICES

FTSE4Good is an investment tool – a series of benchmark and tradable indices designed to aid identification of companies with good records of corporate social responsibility. Launched in July 2001 by FTSE (co-owned by the London Stock Exchange along with the Financial Times), it is the latest in a series of such indices and portfolios, some of which are touched upon earlier in this chapter. It is worthy of mention because FTSE is not itself part of any stock exchange, data vendor or securities house. Its sole business is the creation and calculation of indices and associated services. It is also worthy of note that the indices have been constructed in association with the Ethical Investment Research Service (EIRIS).

Like some of the other organisations in this market, the FTSE4-Good Index Series select companies according to certain criteria which are laid down by the advisory committee and which have been independently researched and determined. In order to qualify for inclusion in an index, a company must not be subject to industry exclusions and must pass the selection criteria. These criteria are based on what FTSE claims are 'internationally accepted codes of conduct and have been ratified through an extensive global market consultation exercise'. The criteria focus on the positive efforts of companies in three areas and are designed to provide clear and achievable targets for companies to use in developing socially responsible policies and practices. It follows from this that a company not presently included in any of the indices may apply to be included if it can demonstrate its compliance with the criteria.

Even to qualify for consideration, a company must be a constituent of one of the FTSE Developed Index or the FTSE All-Share Index. Investment trusts may not apply, nor may companies in excluded industries. Thereafter, each company is screened according to the FTSE4Good selection criteria. Here are the excluded industries:

- Tobacco producers
- Companies providing strategic parts or services for or manufacturing whole nuclear weapons systems
- Companies manufacturing whole weapons systems
- Owners or operators of nuclear power stations and those mining or processing uranium

But unlike some other indices, the FTSE4Good Advisory Committee has said that there may be a removal of exclusions where suitable and substantial performance criteria can be developed with which to replace them. Again the criteria which must be met in order for a company to be included in an index hold no surprises. It must be able to demonstrate a positive approach to environmental sustainability, social issues and stakeholder relations, and human rights.

Environmental sustainablility

FTSE4Good has selected industry sectors which it views to have potentially a high environmental impact:

Agriculture	Mining and quarrying
Airlines	Materials technology
Aluminium smelting	Oil and gas exploration and production
Airports	Pottery, ceramics and glassware
Basic building materials	Pharmaceuticals
Chemical manufacture	Paper manufacture
Civil engineering and construction	Road distribution services
Cleaning products	Rubber
Electricity	Shipping
Forestry and forest products	Supermarkets
Food producers	Steel
Glass	Shipyards
Housebuilders	Vehicle manufacture
Heavy engineering	Water
Integrated oil and gas	Waste disposal
Materials engineering	

Companies in those sectors must be individually reviewed by the advisory committee. Companies in other sectors are automatically considered to have met the selection criteria for environmental sustainability.

Performance will be assessed against 'best practice' by examining the following three items for each company. Indicators have been designed so that results can be scored.

- Environmental policies and commitment
- Environmental management systems
- The environmental reports they have produced in the last three years

There has been some criticism that companies in environment damaging sectors – for example the oil industry – have been included in an index titling itself '4Good'.

Social issues and stakeholder relations

Companies are assessed on the extent to which their annual reports, websites or the information provided in response to a questionnaire which was prepared by EIRIS demonstrates a concern about their relations with stakeholders and influence on society at large. The assessment is based on the best practice framework and performance, and it will cover each company's

- Policies
- Management systems
- Practice/performance on this issue

To qualify for inclusion in the index, companies must disclose information that meets at least two of the requirements laid out in the documentation.

Human rights

The selection criteria involve identification of companies with the greatest responsibility for the maintenance of human rights, and these are defined as companies operating in businesses of strategic importance in countries with the poorest human rights records. The FTSE4Good Advisory Committee will only assess high-impact companies in this area. Companies that are not high impact will be deemed to have met the human rights selection criteria. The performance of these high-impact companies will be assessed against 'best practice', which means having policies that meet any one of the following three conditions on a global basis:

- Have a policy statement specifically on human rights, which goes beyond employee rights.
- Have a policy statement committing to at least two of the International Labour Organisation's Core Labour Standards for employees globally.
- Have signed up to human rights initiatives such as the UN Global Compact, the Global Sullivan Principles, SA 8000, Ethical Trading Initiative, or Voluntary Principles on Security and Human Rights.

Principles are then laid out with which a company must demonstrate compliance, and according to FTSE4Good, 'this model for best practice is gaining acceptance as the best way for companies to address the challenges of corporate social responsibility'.

The entire exercise is, in essence, one of benchmarking but it remains to be seen whether the criteria are sufficiently demanding. FTSE4Good itself says:

> No system of criteria can anticipate every eventuality. The Indices may occasionally include companies who are involved in controversy surrounding the social responsibility of their business practices. From time to time this may give rise to questions about their inclusion in the FTSE4Good Indices.

That could well prove to be a masterly understatement.

RISK ISSUES

Different funds and data collators rely on different information streams, and different funds require different types of information. One relatively common request is in relation to risk issues. Safety and Environmental Risk Management Rating Agency Ltd (SERM) is an example of a rating agency that relies solely on risk in determining whether a company may be regarded as socially responsible. SERM justifies its reliance on risk as 'an overall, balanced assessment of the financial exposure of an organisation to its safety and environmental risks, relative to its ability to manage them and to meet potential liabilities'. The SERM rating process could in theory be useful to companies in helping them to prioritise and manage risks. The rating is determined using a mathematical model which considers the likelihood of potential incidents given the company's risk management systems, and the total costs of such incidents.

However, risk is a much broader issue and therefore requires broader treatment in this chapter. The Institute of Risk Management rates environmental risk in the top five risks that most companies face. In the United States, Mileti and Peek-Gottschlich (Department of Sociology and the Natural Hazards Research and Applications Information Center, University of Colorado) have recently completed a significant piece of work reported in *Risk Management* (Vol. 3, no. 1, pp. 61–70). Intended to take stock of the US relationship to hazards, past, present and most importantly future, the authors outline a comprehensive approach to enhancing society's ability to reduce the costs of disaster. They develop their thesis to show that many disaster losses are the predictable results of interactions between:

- The physical environment
- The social and demographic characteristics of the communities that experience them
- The components of the built environment

The authors are of the view that three principle influences are at work: (1) the Earth's physical systems are constantly changing (climate change provides a good example of this); (2) recent and projected changes in the demographic composition of the US population mean greater exposure to many hazards (e.g. the number of people residing in coastal counties subject to hurricanes is increasing); (3) the built environment from transport systems through communications to homes and office buildings is growing in density, thereby increasing the potential losses from natural forces.

The consequence of this is that disaster losses are growing in the United States. It is estimated by the authors that 80% of the $500 billion (in 1994 dollars) of total dollar losses stem from climatological events, and that only 17% of such losses are insured. The numbers do not include indirect costs such as downtime for business, lost employment, environmental damage or emotional effects on victims. Since there is no single repository for data nor a systematic reporting system, it is apparently impossible to determine losses with a higher degree of accuracy. And so the authors have sought out new means to approach hazards. They are set out here, as they are as valid for those interpreting environmental data as they are for the insurance industry.

Adopt a global systems perspective

Rather than resulting from surprise environmental events, disasters arise from the interaction between the Earth's physical systems, its human systems and its built infrastructure. So, a broad view, which encompasses all three systems and the interactions between them, can enable us to find better solutions.

Accept responsibility for hazards and disasters

We, not nature, are the cause of disaster losses. Such losses stem from choices about when and how human development will proceed. However, there is no total solution to natural hazards, since technology cannot make the world safe from all the forces of nature.

Anticipate ambiguity and change

The view that hazards are relatively static has led to the false conclusion that any mitigation effort is desirable and will in some vague way reduce the grand total of future losses. The reality is that change can occur quickly and non-linearly. Human adaptation to hazards must become as dynamic as the problems presented by the hazards themselves.

Reject short-term thinking

Mitigation as frequently conceived is too short-sighted. In general, people have a cultural and economic predisposition to think primarily in the short term. Sustainable mitigation will require a longer-term view that takes into account the overall effect of mitigation efforts on this and future generations.

Account for social forces

Societal factors, such as how people view hazards and mitigation efforts, or how the free market operates, play a critical role in determining which steps are actually taken and which are overlooked, and thus the extent of future disaster losses. Because such social forces are now known to be much more powerful than disaster specialists previously thought, a growing understanding of physical systems and improved technology cannot suffice. Effectively to address natural hazards, mitigation must become a basic social value.

Enhance sustainable development principles

Disasters are more likely where unsustainable development occurs. Moreover, disasters hinder movement toward sustainablility because, for example, they degrade the environment and undercut the quality of life. Sustainable mitigation activities should strengthen a community's social, economic and environmental resiliency, and vice versa.

The authors (Messrs. Mileti and Peek-Gotlschlich) demonstrate that an array of techniques and tools have evolved over time to assist in coping with losses from hazards and disasters, and while not all are relevant in the context of the environmental themes explored in this book, some are and they are repeated here:

- *Land use*: limit expansion into sensitive areas.
- *Warnings*: short-term forecasts may not reduce property damage but can improve loss of life. Long-term forecasts can reduce property damage but may not improve loss of life.
- *Engineering and building codes*: build to withstand the impact of natural forces. This means first identifying what the natural forces are likely to be, then deciding positively whether it is the right place to build and finally using appropriate building methods.
- *Insurance*: will insurance be available if the company chooses to build the wrong property in the wrong place? Are the right risks covered? Is insurance available for the risks that should be covered?
- *New technology*: not of the type suggested by the authors for hazard mitigation, (but in the context of this book) of the type that will reduce polluting emissions and enhance the quality of the environment.
- *Emergency preparedness and recovery*: in England this is now a part of every application for a Pollution Prevention and Control permit (required for the most polluting industrial processes. And in the United States it contributes to saving lives and injuries, limits property damage and minimises disruption. This enables a quicker recovery.

The authors complete their paper by proposing a model which could act to improve hazard mitigation while retaining the US-driven paradigm that social and technological approaches to mitigation can act overall to reduce the incidence or severity of disastrous events. Jan P. Rockett, director of Rockett Associates Ltd, responding to the paper in the same edition of *Risk Management*, takes a more European approach to the problems identified. His view, and it will strike a chord with many in Europe, is that disasters are the result not of external forces but of how we live our lives and the way we structure our society. As such, he argues, disaster reduction can come about only through fundamental changes in political and social mores.

It seems to us that reducing the principles stated above from the macro US organisation, to the micro organisation of a would-be socially responsible company, is rewarding.

- If instead of a 'global systems perspective' a company views the local physical system, its employees and its built infrastructure, it may avoid potential environmental problems.
- If it will 'accept responsibility for hazards and disasters' rather than indulge in the culture of blame that is so prevalent, and exercise its intellectual capacity to analyse information probably already within its domain, then it will be alert to potential environmental improvements.
- If it will 'anticipate ambiguity and change' then the organisation will become more dynamic and gain a competitive edge over its competitors.
- If it will 'reject short-term thinking' and plan for long-term environmental improvements then sustainable development may result.
- If it will 'account for social forces' then this may overcome the positive screening process referred to at the start of this chapter.
- If it will 'embrace sustainable development principles' then this can only result in environmental benefit.

What results from this rather extended line of argument is that if risk mitigation measures are put in place then losses are reduced, the bottom line improves and the environment benefits.

THE TURNBULL REPORT

No discussion of risk issues will be complete without reference to the Turnbull Guidance for Directors on Corporate Governance issued by the Institute of Chartered Accountants in England and Wales in 1999.[5] The guidance requires directors of UK listed companies to develop a corporate-wide risk management approach to internal control as an integral part of corporate governance policies and systems. Risk management is, of course, an established feature of corporate governance in many areas. However, current practices in investment appraisal, project management, health and safety, and environmental management often lack integration, common guiding principles, and consistency in standards or coverage. Turnbull aims to change this by making directors specifically accountable for developing organisation-wide risk management policies and for implementing integrated, inclusive and dynamic risk management strategies.

The Turnbull Report states that 'a company's system of internal control has a key role in the management of risks that are significant to the fulfilment of its business objectives'. It indicates that the company's internal control system should:

- Be embedded within its operations and not be treated as a separate exercise
- Be able to respond to changing risks within and outside the company
- Enable each company to apply it in an appropriate manner related to its key risks

The guidance requires companies to identify, evaluate and manage their significant risks and to assess the effectiveness of the related internal control system. Boards of directors are called on regularly to review reports on the effectiveness of the system of internal control in managing key risks, and to undertake an annual assessment for the purpose of making their statements on internal control in the annual report. The London Stock Exchange has said that full compliance is required for accounting periods ending on or after 23 December

[5] Its formal title is the Turnbull Report on Internal Control: Guidance for Directors on the Combined Code and Internal Control. The guidance is issued as a result of an agreement between ICAEW and the London Stock Exchange that ICAEW would provide guidance on the Combined Code to assist listed companies to comply with it.

2000. Thus has risk management become an integral part of normal governance processes. The guidance clarifies and prescribes the respective roles of the board, its committees and management in implementing risk management through internal control systems and policies. Boards and managers are now directly accountable to shareholders for the effective management and control of their corporate risk exposures. Thus the guidance goes beyond suggestion (as might be expected of guidance) to definitive interpretation of principle D Z of the Combined Code.[6]

Here are some rquirements of Turnbull:

- Directors must ensure that an organisation-wide risk management policy is formulated then communicated, accepted and implemented as a corporate policy throughout the company.
- Directors are responsible for the implementation of these policies through internal control systems that provide the capacity to monitor the corporate risk environment continuously.
- Directors must ensure periodic effectiveness reviews are carried out to quality-assure the processes.
- Directors are responsible for providing annual reports to shareholders both on the risk policies and on risk management effectiveness.

The appendix to the Report contains a series of broad-ranging questions which boards may wish to consider and discuss with management in applying the guidance. It is helpful to look at some of these questions in relation to environmental issues, specifically the issues in Table 5.6.

With these questions answered, the company may fairly be said to have a risk management policy and the skills to implement it. Accordingly, it must then look to design a corporate risk management strategy and plan. The corporate risk management strategy is intended to implement the measures necessary for determining a reasonable and acceptable level of environmental risk. The plan is for managing the activities of the company so as to avoid exceeding those levels.

[6] In 1991 the Cadbury Committee issued its report on the financial aspects of corporate governance. Cadbury was followed by Greenbury and Hempel. All these recommendations were then reduced by the London Stock Exchange in 1998 into the Combined Code.

There are four essentials to risk management:

- Risk identification
- Risk analysis
- Risk planning
- Risk management

These have to some extent been canvassed earlier in relation to the research carried out by Mileti and Peek-Gottschlich, so all we need note is that they too form part of Turnbull and are an integral part of every environmental management system.

Table 5.6 *Risk management policy: elements for director's consideration*[a]

1	What are the objectives of environmental risk management?[b]
2	What are the nature and extent of the risks facing the company?[c]
3	What is the extent of the risk regarded as acceptable for the company to bear?[d]
4	What are the categories of risk regarded as acceptable for the company to bear?[e]
5	What is the likelihood of the identified risks materialising?[f]
6	What is the company's ability to reduce the incidence and impact of environmental risks that do materialise?[g]
7	What are the costs of implementing particular controls relative to the benefit thereby obtained in managing the related risks?[h]
8	Does the management (below board level) have the necessary skills to identify and evaluate the risks faced by the company?
9	Do the employees have sufficient knowledge, skills, information and authority to establish, operate and monitor the system of internal control?

[a] Source: Adapted from Turnbull for use in environmental situations

[b] Possibly to prevent breaches of authorisations granted for particular purposes, e.g. to prevent exceedances under a water discharge authorisation.

[c] Is the risk one of prosecution for breach of an environmental regulation or simply the possibility of a civil action for damages for nuisance?

[d] Is it acceptable to risk prosecution and save a substantial capital cost on abatement plant to reduce polluting emissions, or will to do so expose the company to loss of reputation or other loss?

[e] Is an environmental risk that affects animals but not humans acceptable?

[f] What is the frequency of Environment Agency inspections?

[g] Is the precautionary principle being properly applied?

[h] The EU provides for the proportionality principle, i.e. the cost of the work must be proportionate to the environmental benefit obtained.

SHAREHOLDER ENGAGEMENT

The final element of socially responsible investing is what has come to be called shareholder engagement. We have already seen that if the fund manager does not approve of some element of corporate governance, he has two alternatives: to withdraw from the company, or to engage the company in meaningful dialogue intended to result in an improvement of the element complained about. Shareholder engagement really comes in two forms: the pension fund trustee with a substantial number of shares at his disposal with which he can command the ear of the company, and the campaigning groups who together muster a sufficient number of shares to be able to table a resolution and attend the company AGM. It is generally recognised that resolutions which are more political in nature seem to attain more media attention. Many resolutions, however, accomplish their goal without much fanfare. But that is to the good; it shows that socially responsible investment can impact on business and that it is possible to effect real, positive change.

During 2000, socially responsible shareholder resolutions in the United States concerning equal opportunity and other employment issues were particularly successful. They included resolutions on disclosure of employment data, sexual-orientation-based discrimination policy, glass ceilings, workplace violence, and policies concerning employees with disabilities. Standardised employment data enables measurement of a company's performance in terms of workplace diversity and the provision of equal employment opportunities. Social investors usually obtain the company's most recent EEO-1 consolidated data form, a one-page worksheet submitted to the federal government by all private companies with one hundred or more employees and all companies that hold federal contracts. This form is said to be the most comprehensive breakdown of workplace diversity data. Companies are not required to release EEO-1 data to the public, and some companies choose not to share the data with investors. Several US companies, the subject of an AGM resolution, subsequently agreed to disclose employment data. They are Bank of America, Morgan Stanley Dean Witter, Worldcom, Alltel, and Nextel Communications.

The US Equal Employment Opportunity Commission takes data from EEO-1 and produces industry statistics. By obtaining this data, not only can social investors compare the last several years and see how a company has made progress, they can also see how their company is doing compared to others in the industry. Walden Asset Management, with Trillium and Calvert Asset Management, filed a resolution with Bank of America which was ultimately withdrawn, but which ensured that Bank of America was 'incredibly responsive' to the request.

A shareholder resolution on policies to eliminate bias based on sexual orientation also accomplished its task. Walden filed the resolution with American International Group, an insurance and financial services company. The resolution was withdrawn when AIG agreed to adopt and implement a written equal employment opportunity policy barring discrimination on the basis of sexual orientation.

A resolution regarding glass ceilings was filed with Newell Rubbermaid by Calvert Asset Management. This was the second time a resolution was filed with Newell on this issue and the resolution was withdrawn upon a promise of cooperation by the company. A resolution regarding workplace violence filed with CVS also achieved its objective.

Calvert also filed a resolution with Diebold regarding equal opportunity for people with disabilities. The resolution was spurred by a lawsuit filed by the National Association for the Blind, which charged that Diebold manufactured automated teller machines (ATMs) that were not accessible for the blind. While the shareholder resolution dealt only with disclosure of information and employment practices, talks between Calvert and Diebold also included company products. Diebold agreed not only to disclose employment data and policies regarding employees with disabilities, but also to equip its ATMs with a headphone jack so that blind people could use the machine with audio instruction.

These examples illustrate that shareholder activism can effectively achieve the dual goals of social investors: doing what is right and increasing shareholder value. They demonstrate that, at any rate in the United States, there is a focused vocal minority of social shareholders[7] ready to persuade companies to do their bidding.

Photo: *Francesca Partridge.*

[7] The Social Investment Forum states that one in eight dollars held with investment institutions are either in ethically screened portfolios or subject to share voting policies that incorporate social responsibility criteria.

CHAPTER 6

The Sustainable Company: Some Case Studies

INTRODUCTION

Having explored some of the issues surrounding socially responsible companies, sustainability and environmental reporting, it is now appropriate to look at a number of companies that have, in addition to the usual business imperatives, the wider community at heart, and to take a view as to whether such laudable aims as have been expressed in the previous chapters actually do impact on the success of the companies. The case studies that follow have all been taken from publicly available documents and without recourse to the companies themselves.

BRISTOL-MYERS SQUIBB

Bristol-Myers Squibb (BMS) describes itself as 'a leading diversified worldwide health and personal care company whose principal businesses are medicines, beauty care, nutritionals and medical devices'. Its mission is 'to extend and enhance human life by providing the highest-quality health and personal care products'. BMS makes various pledges to its stakeholders, broken down into colleagues, suppliers/partners, shareholders and communities as follows:

We pledge excellence in everything we make and market, providing you with the safest, most effective and highest-quality products. We promise to improve our products through innovation, diligent research and development, and an unyielding commitment to be the very best. We pledge personal respect, fair compensation and honest and equitable treatment. To all who qualify for advancement, we will make every effort to provide opportunity. We affirm our commitment to foster a globally diverse workforce and a company-wide culture that encourages excellence, leadership, innovation and a balance between our personal and professional lives. We acknowledge our obligation to provide able and humane leadership and a clean and safe work environment. We pledge courteous, efficient and ethical behaviour and practices; respect for your interests; and an open door. We pledge to build and uphold the trust and goodwill that are the foundation of successful business relationships. We pledge dedication to increasing shareholder value of your company based upon continued profitable growth, strong finances, high productivity and intensive research and development, leading to competitive superiority. We pledge conscientious citizenship, a helping hand for worthwhile causes and constructive action that supports a clean and healthy environment. We pledge Bristol-Myers Squibb to the highest standard of moral and ethical behaviour and to policies and practices that fully embody the responsibility, integrity and decency required of free enterprise if it is to merit and maintain the confidence of our society.

This pledge, first published in 1987, was updated in 1998. It is an important plank of BMS corporate culture and indicates BMS's concern for the interests and expectations of its stakeholders (including the wider world). It is a formal commitment to conscientious citizenship, it supports environmental progress and a safe work environment, and it is expressed to be fully supportive of policies and practices that embody the responsibility, integrity and decency required for free enterprise. Now, these statements set a high moral tone and require no small amount of work and effort to implement. But do the words really add value to the business, and how do they compare with what happens in the hard commercial world in which BMS operates? Moreover, what happens if the pledge is used as a benchmark against which to review BMS operations as disclosed by its various environmental reports and assessments?

Before seeking to answer these questions, it is sensible to look first at the overall purpose of the reports. In the last chapter the authors considered the GRI reporting guidelines. The BMS report was in fact, the first corporate report by a major multinational company to follow the draft GRI guidelines for sustainability reporting, although the report is not, as such, a sustainablility report but an environmental, health and safety progress report with a sustainablility overview. BMS says of the report that it strives to provide stakeholders with factual and balanced information regarding the environmental, social and economic challenges BMS faces, that initiatives have been developed to manage these challenges, and that the report contains information relating to the various stages reached in the implementation of these initiatives.

The report is issued biannually. The authors have used the 1999 Report for the purpose of this case study but as we went to press the 2001 Report was published. It seeks to cover and reflect various topics and issues as follows:

- BMS research and development, manufacturing, and distribution facilities worldwide. Deviations in coverage are noted in the report, together with the rationale behind any differences.
- The data underpinning key environmental health and safety (EHS) aspects of BMS operations.
- BMS EHS policy and goals, and performance against those goals. Performance against voluntary public EHS commitments is also included, as is baseline data for each performance metric.
- Key data items are compared at least over a three-year period, including the baseline year.
- A description of the standard processes for data collection and data reporting.
- Any changes made from one year to the next in the method used to estimate or otherwise determine data.
- The system followed for properly adjusting EHS data to take into account facility acquisitions, divestitures and closings.

- Data is normalised to sales wherever possible and in addition data in absolute terms can be found on the BMS website at www.bms.com/ehs.
- Presentation of data in the report in a way that BMS say is fair and without distortion and in a manner to accommodate the needs of various groups of stakeholders.
- An explanation of significant variations and deviations in performance.

As noted in Chapter 4, scope, period, basis for the report (i.e. whether it is prepared on a going-concern basis, or if not, the basis upon which it was prepared), conservatism and materiality are all matters to be considered in the preparation of a report to conform to GRI Guidelines. Moreover, there should be a statement by the chief executive (in order to demonstrate senior management commitment to the report and its objectives), a profile of the company, a performance summary and performance indicators, the vision of the company and its strategy, the policies of the company, its organisation and management systems and its performance.

It is clear, and indeed unsurprising, that the BMS report more than adequately meets the requirements of the Guidelines. The Chairman in his statement indicated that the BMS focus is on sustainable development. This is defined as 'understanding the economic, social and environmental activities that will enable our generation and future generations to live within the earth's capacities to sustain us'.

BMS addresses sustainable development in the context of its Pledge. As noted, the principles that impel BMS are set out in some detail in the Pledge, and the report both expresses a commitment to achieving those goals and acknowledges the ultimate question posed earlier in this book, Can industrial activity with its primary focus on profit and regulated by fallible government be compatible with sustainable development? In his introduction to the report, the Vice President for EHS implicitly accepts that there is a real dichotomy posed by the aspirations for sustainable development set against the aspirations for business, but he indicates that while BMS alone cannot deal with all the sustainability issues faced by the world, it can and will make its contribution to the resolution of commonly shared economic, social and environmental challenges on a local, regional and global basis, and encourage others to do the same. Perhaps this statement rather begs the question of whether differences between the imperatives of business and sustainable development can be reconciled, but at least there is an acknowledgement of the underlying problem.

BMS has four current goals as set out in the report:

1. Zero work-related illnesses and injuries (and as an interim goal, reduction to levels comparable to those of companies whose safety records are in the top 25% of similar industries).

It is probably not unreasonable to assert that a target of zero accidents is unrealistic, although not uncommon, and that notwithstanding a natural inclination to be risk adverse, companies that claim this target as the ultimate are deceiving themselves and their audience as to any probable likelihood of success in achievement. The authors base this assertion on the fact that not all accidents at work fall under the control of an employer, for example road accidents where the employer's driver is not at fault. Moreover, it is also not unreasonable, bearing in mind the high aspirations of the Pledge, to expect BMS to aspire to a desire more arduous than just to be in the top 25% of companies in the industry sector.

2. Management systems in place to meet BMS EHS codes of practice which are based on Business Charter for Sustainable Development

The BMS management system provides a structure for implementation of sustainable business practices (Figure 6.1).

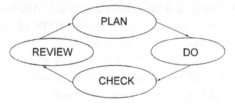

Figure 6.1. *The conventional virtuous circle of environmental management systems*

Compare this with the model which BMS term as their EMS Performance Engine (Figure 6.2).

BMS has structured an individual environmental management system which equals or exceeds the requirements of ISO 14001 (page 171). It is founded upon the 16 principles of the ICC Business

Figure 6.2. *EHS Performance Engine*

Charter (see box 6.1.) and supported by the pledge, EHS policy, guidance, best practice databases, management system self-assessment, opening results and feedback mechanisms. It adds up to a comprehensive system designed to point up the failures in performance as well as to track the improvements.

3. To purchase by the end of 2001 for the purpose of long-term preservation biologically diverse land at least equal to the amount of land occupied by BMS operations worldwide

This goal is plainly a demonstration of the commitment BMS has to the wider environment and to the socially responsible principles it espouses. It will be interesting to look in future years at this project and to determine its value in social and environmental terms.

4. To complete product life cycle reviews of the major products and incorporate life cycle criteria into new product development.

BMS states that life cycle reviews of all existing products have been completed. The financial results are dealt with in the following section, but note that in pure EHS terms, BMS claims significant product improvements. It was intended that the incorporation of life cycle techniques into new product development would be completed by the end of 2000 but there is no readily available evidence yet that this goal has been achieved.

Financial aspects

EHS performance is linked to the overall financial performance of BMS. Traditional financial analysis approaches are adapted for use in calculating the costs, benefits and return on investment of the EHS initiatives in order the better to improve tools and processes; BMS has participated in a number of initiatives related to full cost accounting. Meanwhile, it is possible to extract various figures from the published reports and accounts and to attempt to draw certain conclusions:

- Potential savings of $7,000,000 have been identified in relation to product life cycle techniques. It should, however, be noted that this is said to be an identifiable saving, not an actual one, and in a different part of the EHS report the reference to the saving is qualified by indicating that such saving is over a five-year period.
- Packaging initiatives – simply changing a square bottle to an oval bottle – has resulted in savings of $100,000 in reduced energy use for sterilisation (as sterilisation can take place at a lower temperature) and fewer discards, together with a further $32,000 for the amount of corrugate used for the packing cases. The weight of cartonboard was reduced, resulting in a saving of $140,000, and the cutting guides were changed from a poly-art material to an index stock, saving $60,000
- While use of water remains flat and energy use is reducing, direct financial information with respect thereto is not available. This is sad, as it is an opportunity missed, to demonstrate the direct effect (if any) of environmental measures on the financial bottom line.

And so to return to the questions posed earlier in this case study:

- Do the words really add value to the business? The answer to this question has to be a qualified 'yes'. BMS obviously prizes its EHS policy and strives hard to implement it. There are savings made as a result of the policy and probably much greater savings than BMS actually discloses in terms that are easy to understand and to find in its published documents. However, there is a reason for this. GRI says that absolute values should be given for the indicators, but also suggests that the data should be normalised by company turnover, number of employees or floor space to put them into perspective and allow comparison.
- How do the pledge and other promises made by BMS compare with what happens in the hard commercial world in which BMS operates? In the authors' view it gives BMS a competitive edge of which it can be justly proud. It has a cost, in terms of manpower

for the EHS department, but compliance plus, towards which BMS is currently working, must reduce exposure to unwitting breaches of environmental and health and safely regulations, and foster a relationship with local communities and other stakeholders which others can only admire.

- How does the EHS report stand up if the pledge is used as a benchmark against which to review BMS operations? It seems to the authors that all the principal promises referred to in the pledge are addressed in the report, although there have been varying degrees of success as some issues remain outstanding, on some progress is still being made whilst on others the objectives in the pledge have been accomplished. Moreover, the $100,000,000 five-year programme to assist alleviation of AIDS/HIV in Southern Africa while not part of the EHS campaign, is most certainly part of the socially responsible issues to which the reader was directed in Chapter 5 and which encompass part of the wider view of sustainable development. In relation to AIDS, BMS has perhaps shown the way to other drug companies whose legal action in South Africa in relation to the manufacture of drugs in breach of patents has been withdrawn. The BMS programme is intended to facilitate medical research, promote further education and focus on practical and sustainable solutions.

But the review of BMS is not yet complete. For not only is it the first company to have used the GRI reporting guidelines but it is also named by Dow Jones Sustainability Group Index (DJSGI) as the pharmaceutical industry leader in corporate sustainability performance. The DJSGI were launched in September 1999 jointly with Sustainable Asset Management (SAM) and they were the world's first indexes to track the performance of sustainability-driven companies (see page 122).

The DJSGI were created to address increasing investor interest in companies committed to corporate sustainability principles. These principles include innovative technology, corporate governance, shareholder relations, industrial leadership, and social well-being – all key to BMS corporate values. The indexes are based on a systematic methodology for identifying leading sustainability-driven companies worldwide. The DJSGI include over 200 companies and represent the top 10%, by number of companies, of the leading sustainability companies in 73 industry groups in 33 countries. The DJSGI have a total market capitalisation of approximately $4.3 trillion.

The DJSGI Corporate Sustainability Assessment is the core of the DJSGI index methodology. In 1999 BMS achieved the highest corporate sustainability performance score on the assessment (58.77 out of a maximum score of 74).

ICI

Like BMS, ICI has a venerable history. It employs over 48,000 people and is headquartered in London. The roots of some of the businesses which comprised ICI are to be found in the Industrial Revolution of the nineteenth century. These companies can trace their ancestry back to the earliest days of industry, which brought the discoveries of the laboratory into everyday products. However, the ICI of today has largely set aside its industrial heritage. It describes itself as 'a world leader in manufacturing and supplying ingredients for foods and personal care, specialty polymers, electronic materials, fragrances and flavours'.

The only significant part of the original core business to be retained is the paints division, and ICI is now regarded as a major player in the worldwide development of sensory products. ICI has demonstrated an ability to meet the changing needs of an increasingly global marketplace by rebuilding its portfolio to one based on intellectual capital Since 1997 the company has divested itself of more than 40 businesses such as polyurethanes, Tioxide, petrochemicals, acrylics and fluoropolymers, fetching some £6.1 billion. In their place, the company acquired $8 billion of assets – most notably National Starch, the world's largest industrial adhesives and specialty starch producer, and Quest, a leading fragrance, foods and flavours manufacturer – and from there continued a significant shift to the lighter, higher added value end of the chemicals sector.

This shift has reduced ICI's environmental footprint and in 1997 it began a major review of safety, health and the environment, culminating in the launch of a new set of five-year performance improvement targets called 'Challenge 2005'.

145

ICI safety, security, health and environment (SSHE) policy

The ICI Group will ensure that its activities are conducted safely; the health of its employees, its customers and the public will be protected; environmental performance will meet contemporary requirements; its operations are run in a manner acceptable to local communities; employees, capital, information and other assets will be protected from deliberate harm, damage or loss.

In particular the ICI Group will:

1. Comply with relevant laws and regulations and take any additional measures considered necessary.
2. Ensure that all activities are conducted in a manner consistent with ICI Group Safety, Security, Health and Environmental Standards.
3. Set demanding targets and measure progress to ensure continuous improvement in safety, security, health and environmental performance.
4. Require every member of staff, and those who work on our behalf, to exercise personal responsibility in preventing harm to themselves, others and the environment, and enable them to contribute to every aspect of safety, security, health and environmental protection.
5. Manufacture only those products that can be transported, stored, used and disposed of safely.
6. Seek to develop new or modified products which assist in conserving the environment and lead to sustainable development.
7. Provide appropriate safety, security, health and environmental training and information for all staff.
8. Provide appropriate safety, security, health and environmental information for all contractors and others who work with us, handle our products or operate our technologies.
9. Communicate openly on the nature of our activities, encourage dialogue and report progress on our safety, security, health and environmental performance.
10. Promote the interchange of safety, security, health and environmental information and technology throughout the ICI Group and make our expertise and knowledge available to relevant statutory authorities.

11. Encourage, through positive interaction within the industry, the worldwide development and implementation of the principles of the Chemical Industries' 'Responsible Care' initiative and the International Chamber of Commerce's 'Business Charter for Sustainable Development'.
12. Regularly monitor the application of this SSHE policy.

This policy applies throughout ICI and its subsidiaries worldwide. ICI states that it encourages its related companies to adopt policies which accord with the safety, security, health and environment (SSHE) policy. In its latest environmental report (published 2000 for the year 1999), ICI has reported achieving its targets; and in four out of the five targets it set itself in 1995, it reports that it exceeded those targets. However, over the same period, and as already noted ICI has been transformed beyond recognition from a major producer of bulk chemicals into a specialty products and paints business. Thus it has required a significant amount of informed guesswork to calculate the impact of its new businesses from the 1995 baseline. ICI acknowledges that new targets are needed accurately to reflect the impacts of its new businesses and those targets have been established for the period to 2005; they are reviewed in greater detail later in this section.

ICI was the first company in the chemical industry to approach environmental issues by reference to the environmental burden they created, and it reflected this approach in reporting its emissions data to take account of environmental impacts. But it is to be noted that the new approach followed ICI's significant failure to meet its own targets set in 1990. For example, ICI only just achieved half of the planned reduction of waste output in the five years to 1995 and that included savings achieved by divesting some of the businesses. So some would argue that such radical rethinking was essential.

The targets set in 1996 were intended to halve ICI's environmental burden in four key categories by the end of 2000: acidity to air and water, hazardous air emissions, aquatic oxygen demand (AOD) and aquatic ecotoxicity. ICI also pledged to raise its energy efficiency by 10%. As to exceeding four out of five targets, the performance figures are as follows. Acidity has been cut by 84%, hazardous air emissions by 51%, aquatic ecotoxicity by 50% and improved energy efficiency by 12%. However, it has achieved only a 19% cut in AOD so far, and accepts that its target may not be capable of fulfilment.

It is though, difficult to treat this data as reliable. While the report says that ICI's policy is to make clear the extent of changes in its releases which were due to acquisitions and divestments by altering each year's data back to the baseline, it manifestly fails to say that ICI is still in the process of precisely determining the impacts of the past five years' business changes. According to Dr Frank Rose, vice president for SSHE, 'The change in ICI is enormous in terms of the size, number and complexity of businesses that have gone and those that have come in.'

The difficulty that has arisen is not so much in terms of the businesses sold – that is simply a matter of removing their impact from the data – but of incorporating the data from the businesses acquired, where those businesses either did not have relevant data or had different means or timescales for such measurements. KPMG is the consultancy instructed by ICI to verify the efficacy of the 'letter of assurance' process by which each of the ICI businesses must report annually on its performance to the ICI board. It notes that in some recently acquired businesses where management systems are still being aligned with ICI policies and standards, the letter of assurance process is not as well supported as in other businesses with more mature systems. KPMG has been asked to carry out a comprehensive audit of ICI's management practices and data in order to provide a fully verified account for next year's environmental report, which will reveal the final performance against ICI's targets.

The report goes into some detail on ICI's calculation of energy efficiency, describing its new methodology which eliminates changes in efficiency due to changes in product mix. However, there is no way of ascribing a financial value to the reductions made, which for our purposes, is unfortunate.

Of course, providing a factually accurate picture of its performance following the revamp of the business in 1997, is only part of the story. ICI recognised that the targets it set itself in 1996, when it had a dirtier, more hazardous bulk chemicals business, have far less relevance for its new businesses. New targets, reflecting the new businesses, were needed from 2000 and these have now been published.

In addition to the SSHE policy, ICI also makes a number of

promises. These do not appear to have the same type of board support as the BMS pledge, but they are worth setting out:

The principles by which we operate, within the limits of current knowledge are:

- All work-related injuries and illnesses are preventable. Our goal is zero harm.
- All escapes of hazardous materials can be prevented and emissions in the course of operation will progressively be reduced towards zero.
- We will adhere to the highest standards for the safe disposal of waste materials.
- Energy, water and resources, both natural and man-made, will be utilised efficiently. We will minimise waste.
- New products can be developed which have increasing margins of safety for users and the environment throughout their life cycle.
- Line management is accountable for leading the continuous improvement in SHE performance to defined goals.
- Everyone has a personal responsibility for their own safety and health, for others in the workplace and for the environment in which they work. Safety and good health are equally important away from work and will be encouraged.
- Everyone should be involved in the SHE improvement process.
- ICI contractor SHE performance will be managed by them to the same standards.
- Information on SHE performance will be made available to those around us.

It seems to the authors that there are a plethora of statements, both of policy and of good intention, which are confusing. The Responsible Care System introduced in 1999 includes security, the promises made above do not seem to do so. Moreover, while board-level responsibility is identified for health, safety and the environment, a member of the executive team has responsibility for human resources. The Responsible Care System includes product stewardship and a model is used to identify the life cycle impacts of products and assess opportunities to reduce them. Ninety business units out of a total of 112 that might benefit have implemented the programme and it has resulted in improvements, for example, in the design of glass bottles. However, no cost savings have been publicly identified as a result of using the model.

Where ICI really scores from an environmental standpoint is in relation to its Nature Link programme. All ICI sites larger than 10 hectares or located close to sensitive biodiversity regions are undertaking an ecology survey and developing a management plan; this objective complements the Nature Link programme of assessment which has been running since the early 1990s. More than 2,500 species of animals, birds, insects and plants found at 86 sites in 23 countries have been made available to a global audience through a dedicated website. The programme provides expertise in ecology and conservation management, as well as funding, to assist in the creation and enhancement of wildlife habitats adjacent to ICI facilities.

Financial aspects

Unfortunately, there is no financial information contained in the SHE report and no easily identifiable information in the financial accounts. Moreover, although it is well known that ICI has some environmental legacies, these are not described. It is understood that on the sale of each business, ICI identified its liabilities and retained responsibility for them. After publication of the 2000 accounts, ICI offered to buy back houses built on contaminated land; the cost of that is not (nor should be) disclosed in the last accounts. However, and bearing in mind the requirements set out in FRS 12, it might have been expected that some reserve would have been made or a note appended. It is of course possible that provision has been made, but that it is not readily recognisable as such. It will be interesting to see how the issue is treated in the 2001 accounts.[1]

Three questions were posed in relation to BMS and it is worth posing them in relation to ICI:

[1] In 1993 ICI started investigations in the village of Weston in north-west England, looking at the possible effects of over a hundred years' chemical manufacturing in the area. In 2000 ICI found that traces of a chemical from a long-disused waste disposal site had the potential to affect some neighbouring properties. ICI then started an extensive and thorough technical investigation and introduced a range of support policies to help local residents. As a result of the investigations, ICI has been able to confirm that the majority of Weston village is not at risk and ICI continues to work in partnership with residents and the local authority to resolve the situation. Although it is not here reported, ICI has offered the buyback referred to above.

- Do the words used in the policy and in other statements really add value to the business? Again the answer must be a qualified 'yes'. No company can afford to ignore environmental or sustainability issues. ICI has plainly struggled with its environmental heritage. It was engaged in the heavy chemicals industry at a time before the effects of various industrial processes were understood in terms of their long-term environmental disbenefits. Nevertheless, it is also plain that there are differences between one set of statements and values produced by ICI, and another. There are also differences in the level of responsibility governing different groupings. In a company that expresses its targets in terms of employees, it is notable that responsibility for human resources is not at board level. Moreover, there is a certain lack of consistency and what appears to be real commitment, although the reason for that may be the fundamental shift which has occurred in the business in the last four years. However, if ICI wishes to reach the top echelons of environmental performance and sustainable development, it seems to the authors that there is still progress to be made.
- How do the policy and other promises made by ICI compare with what happens in the hard commercial world in which ICI operates? It is very difficult to answer this question. There is much information publicly available, but ICI has perhaps not been fully frank in its annual report. At least one prosecution has gone unreported there, although it has received mention in the specialist environmental press, and if such good progress is being made with respect to the product stewardship programme then the authors would have expected the financial numbers associated therewith to have been reported.
- How does the SSHE report stand up if the policy is used as a benchmark against which to review ICI operations? This is also a difficult question to answer in 2001. With the change in emphasis of the business, it is hard to establish the actual targets and the actual performance. ICI does say that, in its view, a sustainable society stands the best chance of achieving steady economic growth and that regulation and taxation will increasingly be weighted towards achieving sustainability. In order to help define the ICI contribution to these issues and to address the complex subject of sustainable development, ICI is working with the World

Business Council for Sustainable Development and Forum for the Future. However, the only constructive comment right now is that the jury is out but will return with a verdict when there are accurate measurements on the effects of the changes made in the businesses of ICI.

And the review of ICI does not end here. For like BMS there has already been independent comment. ICI does not figure significantly as a best performer, but it has retained its top ranking for the fourth consecutive year in a league table of the way UK companies manage environmental matters. This is the index organised by Business and the Environment, a campaign run by the charity Business in the Community to measure how effectively companies minimise the impact of their operations on the environment. ICI secured 85% overall against a national average of 73%, and it achieved a 99% score in the chemicals sector compared with an average of 70%.

UBS

The Swiss Bank Corporation, now part of UBS AG, was established in 1872 as Basler Bankverein, specialising in investment banking. In 1895 the name was changed to Basler und Zürcher Bankverein when it merged with Zürcher Bankverein. At that time the bank also began commercial banking. After absorbing two other Swiss banks in 1897, it adopted its present name of UBS. Since that time there have been a number of additional absorptions and acquisitions, and branches and representative offices have been opened in Switzerland and in other countries. SBC merged with Union Bank of Switzerland in 1998 and the group, now known as UBS AG, is one of the top ten banks in the world.

UBS is the world's largest global asset manager, a top-tier provider of investment banking and securities distribution, and a leading provider of private banking services. In Switzerland, UBS is the undoubted market leader, serving more than 4 million personal and corporate clients. The financial stability of UBS is borne out by credit ratings consistently among the highest of any bank. In 1999 it managed assets totalling $1,064 billion. UBS says it sustains growth by integrating its strengths, allowing it to take advantage of global trends in personal wealth and securities investment, and to deliver greater benefits to its clients. The businesses of UBS operate from major centres in Zurich, London, New York, Chicago, Singapore and Tokyo, plus a total of 95 locations in over 50 countries. Following the November 2000 merger with PaineWebber (now UBS Paine-Webber), the group employs some 70,000 people worldwide.

In banking, UBS seeks to create shareholder value by taking advantage of environmental opportunities in the market. UBS has developed a number of investment products which target clients who are concerned to make socially responsible investment. The assets UBS manages in line with environmental and social criteria totalled CHF 755 million in June 2000. One of its funds invests in stocks which achieve an above-average rating from an environmental, social and financial perspective. UBS assesses potential investees on the basis of eco-efficiency plus social criteria such as human rights, armaments, internalisation of external costs, insurability of risks and communication with employees and society.

UBS has said that in future the analysis will include additional aspects concerning social policy, codes of conduct, business in developing countries, and employee support and involvement. Environmental risks are also factored into the risk management processes of UBS, particularly in the areas of credit policy and investment banking. In 1999 UBS Warburg approved a Global Environmental Risk Policy, setting out principles to be considered in the financial commitment and credit processes. UBS Warburg is one of the first investment banks to approve such a policy.

UBS has indicated that it wishes to contribute towards ensuring sustainable development, and an active environmental policy is part of the financial group's responsibility towards future generations. UBS acknowledges its responsibility to all its stakeholders and has said that it will provide its clients with superior value-added financial services, generate sustainable returns for its shareholders, be an attractive employer for those who work for it, and meet its responsibilities as a good citizen within the community. Thus UBS embraces the fundamental tenets of the socially responsible company.

The BMS and ICI case studies concentrated on industrial companies, one centred in the US, the other in the UK. UBS as a service company within the European Free Trade Area (EFTA), not the

European Union, brings a third dimension to this discussion. It is of course easier for a service company to control its emissions, wastes and energy consumption than it is for manufacturing industry, but nevertheless the task is considerable in an organisation the size of UBS. Like both BMS and ICI, UBS makes various statements with respect to its environmental policies. The executive board made the following statement in 1998:

Environmental protection is one of the most pressing issues facing our world today. Consequently environmental issues are a challenge for all companies in all sectors. UBS regards sustainable development as a fundamental aspect of sound business management and was one of the first banks to sign the United Nations Environment Programme's 'Statement by Financial Institutions on the Environment and Sustainable Development'.

And at the same time it published its current environmental policy:

Banking, financial products and services

We seek to build shareholder value by taking advantage of environmental market opportunities. At the same time, we will incorporate due consideration of environmental risks into our risk management processes, especially in lending and investment banking.

Operations

We will actively seek ways of reducing the environmental impact to air, soil and water from our in-house operations. The main focus is the reduction of greenhouse gas emissions.

Management

We seek to ensure the efficient implementation of our environmental policy via an environmental management system which includes sound objectives, programs and monitoring. We ensure compliance with regulatory requirements and furthermore, we integrate environmental aspects in internal communication and training. We welcome open dialogue and communicate actively with all relevant stakeholders.

The implementation of this environmental policy is a process of continuous improvement which will take several years to complete. Although many goals have already been achieved, there are still areas which need to be addressed. The content of this policy will be reviewed periodically by the management.

In addition, UBS supports the principles of the UN's Global Compact initiative, and has ratified a group-wide environmental policy focusing on banking, in-house ecology and environmental management. In fact, environmental management has a long history at UBS Starting with the optimisation of its own operations (energy, purchase, waste), environmental management has been extended to include bank products and services.

In 1978 the first energy functional unit was established; this was followed by the formal energy guidelines, an environmental strategy (1991), environmental performance evaluations for Zurich, the signing of the UNEP bank declaration, the signing of the ICC Charter for Sustainable Development, (see box 6.1) and the first in-house ecology analyses. There then followed an environmental credit assessment procedure for Swiss corporate clients, the first environmental report, purchasing guidelines for office ecology and the environmental training functional unit. Then came environmental equity analyses for investment advisory services, a brochure entitled 'Environmental management for building construction projects', the Eco-Performance-Portfolio Funds, Cooperation on the Environmental Management in Financial Institutions guidelines, published by the Swiss Bankers Association (SBA), and in 1998 a new organisation and environmental policy at UBS, which is accredited under ISO 14001.

Hand in hand with internal environmental improvements came a recognition by UBS that environmental best practices form a tool for evaluating investees and customers of the bank. So UBS considers a number of decisive factors in acquiring new client assets, including the financial performance of products, the level of service offered and the company's reputation. Environmental and social aspects are incorporated into its company research, and this is becoming more and more important, particularly for institutional investors such as pension funds. UBS looks at how a company's strategies, processes and products impact on its financial success and the environment, and what contribution these elements make to the company and its employees.

The shares selected are shares in companies which can demonstrate long-term success and which generate sustainable financial revenues, but as alluded to earlier, ecological funds have another important function for UBS: they ensure that the know-how needed for the sustainability analysis is strengthened within UBS itself and the product is continuously expanded and improved. The development and integration of an individual method of analysing a company according to environmental and social aspects in asset management means that it can recognise environmentally oriented investment products.

The first part of this book looked at the reasons for, and the effects of, climate change. Recognising that this is one of the most important issues faced by the world today, UBS views the Kyoto Protocol as a business incentive for reducing greenhouse gas levels. The Kyoto Protocol proposes a system whereby emission certificates can be issued. A company which emits greenhouse gases has two options: it can either reduce its emission levels and then sell the certificates which it no longer requires, or it can continue to emit the same level of gases. In the latter instance, the company would have to buy additional certificates, since the emission levels permitted per certificate will be reduced progressively. This will give rise to emissions trading and turn the certificates themselves into a form of security.

Following a thorough analysis of its own business and the ecological mechanisms of the Kyoto Protocol, UBS has put in place a basic structure for examining the possible launch of a globally diversified portfolio of projects aimed at reducing greenhouse gases. Investors will profit from the income generated by trading in emissions certificates. It has also led UBS to appreciate that the more efficiently and sparingly it uses its resources and hence reduces emission levels, the less it will have to pay in terms of costs. Energy management and in-house ecology enhance operating margins.

Even a service provider like UBS has environmental risks to contend with in-house, for example, from the storage of chemical materials or when operating heating or IT systems. It takes care of these and other risks through its environmental management system. Compliance with legal requirements is a fundamental part of ISO 14001 since no company can be accredited without undertaking, as a minimum, to comply with existing legislation and regulation. UBS states that compliance audits regularly form part of its internal and external checks, not least because they are one of the main prerequisites for retaining ISO 14001 certification. Brochures are an important means by which IBS informs its employees about how to handle risks correctly; they contain concrete instructions on what to do. With these print media in the areas of environmental protection, environmental law and safety at work, UBS is striving for more than just compliance with legal requirements. Tips and standards help to reduce risks further and save costs.

Box 6.1
ICC Business Charter for Sustainable Development: Principles for Environmental Management

Corporate priority: to recognise environmental management as among the highest corporate priorities and as a key determinant to sustainable development, to establish policies, programmes and practices for conducting operations in an environmentally sound manner.

Integrated management: to integrate these policies, programmes and practices fully into each business as an essential element of management in all its functions.

Process of improvement: to continue to improve corporate policies, programmes and environmental performance, taking into account technical developments, scientific understanding, consumer needs and community expectation, with legal regulations as a starting point and to apply the same environmental criteria internationally.

Employee education: to educate, train and motivate employees to conduct their activities in an environmentally responsible manner.

Prior assessment: to assess environmental impacts before starting a new activity or project or before decommissioning a facility or leaving a site.

Products and services: to develop and provide products and services that have no undue environmental impact and are safe in their intended use, that are efficient in their consumption of energy and natural resources, and that can be recycled, reused or disposed of safely.

Customer advice: to advise and where relevant educate customers, distributors and the public in the safe use, transportation storage and disposal of products provided, and to apply similar considerations to the provision of services.

Facilities and operations: to develop, design, research and operate facilities and conduct activities taking into consideration the efficient use of energy and raw materials, the sustainable use of renewable resources, the minimisation of adverse environmental impact, and waste generation and the safe and responsible disposal of residual wastes.

Research: to conduct or support research on the environmental impacts of raw materials, products, processes, emissions and waste associated with the enterprise and on the means of minimising such adverse impacts.

Precautionary approach: to modify the manufacture, marketing or use of products or services to the conduct of activities, consistent with scientific and technical understanding, to prevent serious or irreversible environmental degradation.

Contractors and suppliers: to promote the adoption of these principles by contractors acting on behalf of the enterprise, encouraging and where appropriate requiring improvements in their practices to make them consistent with those of the enterprise and to encourage the wider adoption of these principles by suppliers.

Emergency preparedness: to develop and maintain where appropriate hazards exist, emergency preparedness plans in conjunction with the emergency services, relevant authorities and the local community, recognising potential cross-boundary impacts.

Transfer of technology: to contribute to the transfer of environmentally sound technology and management methods throughout the industrial and public sectors.

Contributing to the common effort: to contribute to the development of public policy and to business, governmental and intergovernmental programmes and educational initiatives that will enhance environmental awareness and protection.

Openness to concerns: to foster openness and dialogue with employees and the public anticipating and responding to their concerns about the potential hazards and impacts of operations, products, wastes or services, including those of transboundary or global significance.

Compliance and reporting: to measure environmental performance, to conduct regular environmental audits and assessments of compliance with company requirements and these principles, and periodically to provide appropriate information to the board of directors, shareholders, employees, the authorities and the public.

Financial aspects

Following the deregulation of the Swiss energy market, UBS conducted a survey that provided it with statistics on consumption (broken down into energy produced internally and energy provided by outside suppliers), the various tariffs charged at specific times of day and during each season, and the substantial price differences which exist between the different UBS locations.

This analysis showed that the deregulated market brought UBS lower prices and improved services. However, UBS sensibly recognises there is a danger that these lower prices result in efficient energy consumption being perceived as less of a priority. A further danger identified is a possible decline in the proportion of energy taken from renewable sources, up to now around 60%. This change would lead to a significant deterioration in UBS's environmental performance evaluation, even if consumption levels remained stable (Figure 6.3).

At the end of 1999 UBS chose the supplier with the best price/ performance ratio. The advantages brought by this solution on the business side are lower energy prices, price models that are transparent and straightforward, and heavily streamlined payments

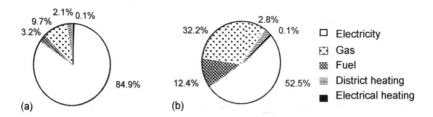

Figure 6.3. *Energy sources as a percentage*

processes. Moreover, it decided that stringent action was necessary to reduce energy consumption. It therefore looked at its computer systems – the heart of its business. If they are hooked up to a network, many office installations such as PCs, monitors, printers and other electronic devices use energy even if they are not actively used. As well as consuming energy needlessly, they generate heat, which in turn puts greater pressure on air-conditioning systems.

These machines can also exacerbate system overloads at peak times, which can lead to outages on servers and other systems. So an energy-efficient low-impact power supply was deemed necessary for LCD monitors. A manufacturer was identified and the screens built. This monitor costs less than CHF 25 more than a monitor with a conventional power supply. While a conventional power supply consumes between 4 and 7 watts in sleep mode or when switched off, a device incorporating the best technology can consume up to 10 times less. Turned into hard statistics, UBS saved 1.6 million kilowatt-hours of energy in Switzerland alone, equivalent to the average annual consumption of 350 Swiss households

UBS had certain targets for 2000 which cannot yet be reviewed against actual performance. It is, however, possible to draw certain conclusions from them:

- Stabilise the area-specific total energy usage at 240 kW/m^2.
- Reduce water consumption per employee by 10%.
- Reduce the fuel consumption per 100 km of UBS delivery vehicles by an average of 5% (based on 14 litres per 100 km in 1997).
- Reduce the fuel consumption per 100 km of UBS cars by an average of 5% (based on 11 litres per 100 km in 1997).

- Reduce by 10% the environmental impact resulting indirectly from paper consumption.
- Reduce the amount of waste produced per employee from 325 kg in 1997 to 275 kg by 2003, a reduction of 15%.
- The 60% recycling quota for 1997 will be increased to 75% by 2003.
- Wherever possible, to use recognised construction ecology instruments (e.g. the guidelines outlined in 'Environmental Management of Building Construction Projects', IPB building ecology recommendations, etc.) for construction projects (new buildings, renovations, etc.).

Moreover, by now an assessment should have been made of the extent to which all the materials used and stored (cleaning materials, chemicals, etc.) harm the environment. And ecological grading of the 30% of office consumables with the highest turnover should have taken place, together with ecological improvement of each class of materials in the range.

And the conclusions, of course, are that some of these measures, if properly implemented, will result in significant cost savings and the rest should improve the environment even if no direct cost savings are attached. These targets do demonstrate that environmental management systems produce a need for continuous improvement. For once these targets are achieved, ISO 14001 dictates that there must be a further round of improvements.

It is now appropriate to return to the three questions posed in each of the previous case studies:

- Do the words really add value to the business? The answer to this question is an unqualified "yes". UBS has taken environmental concerns and used them internally to drive down costs and externally to add value to its business and as a means of identifying good performers. Like BMS, UBS obviously prizes its EHS policy and strives hard to implement it. A top-down approach appears to be in force so that the culture of environmental improvement is to be found throughout the organisation. UBS's published documents are easy to understand and it is easy to identify where savings can be and are being made. This results in a set of figures that the average interested investor can comprehend and relate to. Of course, a service industry has far fewer environmental problems with which to contend than traditional manufacturing industry but that should not detract from the scale of success enjoyed by UBS.

- How do the policy and other promises made by UBS compare with what happens in the hard commercial world in which UBS operates? In the authors' view the conclusion is identical to that reached for BMS. It gives UBS a competitive edge of which UBS can be justly proud. It has a cost, in terms of manpower for the EHS department, but compliance must reduce exposure to unwitting breaches of environmental and health and safely regulations, and foster a relationship with employees and other stakeholders which others can only admire.

- How does the environmental report stand up if the various promises and statements are used as a benchmark against which to review UBS operations? It seems to the authors that good progress is being made on all fronts. The authors are particularly impressed with the double edge that UBS has given to environmental management. To use internal information and methodology to determine the worthiness of potential investees or borrowers has to be a financially effective way of doubling value at little extra cost. It also has to be said that there is little likelihood of any company persuading UBS that it is more environmentally efficient than it actually is. However, while UBS has been in the forefront of sustainable banking practices, it has no substantial contribution to offer to the wider community in terms of the BMS AIDS programme or the ICI ecology programme. UBS is a Dow Jones Sustainability Group Index company, one of a group that includes another Swiss bank, Credit Suisse, which presently occupies the number one position.

What is not evident from the environmental report or from the accounts, is whether there is an environmental spend that can be separately identified. This is disappointing because if there is to be a demonstration of the benefits of environmental improvement that has a tangible effect on the financial bottom line, then there must be a simple means to demonstrate the benefits. That is not in evidence; at any rate, the authors could not identify it in this company.

CHAPTER 7
How to Identify a Strong Performer

INTRODUCTION

How does an investor go about identifying what, if any, economic value has been accrued by a company when it states that it has integrated business and environmental values? There is no easy answer to this question. Chapter 4 dealt with one aspect of this issue, its focus on environmental reporting and accounting. This chapter provides an insight into why the environment is potentially so important to business and examines how investors can discriminate between good, bad and indifferent environmental performers.

It opens with an examination of how environmental issues have spurred the development of new technology that has in turn spawned potentially massive new markets. The selected case studies focus on renewable energy and the automotive industry. But the point is made that the environment will continue to force the pace of innovation and provide opportunities for investors prepared to support enterprises bringing new environmental technology onto the market.

At the other end of the scale, a relatively recent addition to management's range of techniques to increase efficiency is examined in detail. Certified environmental management systems have been around for a little over half a decade and in that time they have acquired a somewhat mixed reputation. Intended to provide organisations with a framework to balance and integrate economic and environmental interests and achieve competitive advantages, EMS have not stopped some companies from appearing in court. This chapter describes how EMS came about, examines the basic EMS building blocks and discusses the benefits of implementation. It balances this with some examples where EMS have not performed to expectations.

Finally, it examines how companies can help themselves attract investment by improving their communications. In doing so, it moves on from Chapter 5 and looks in more detail at the difficulties of presenting meaningful environmental accounts.

THE ENVIRONMENT: SPURRING THE NEXT REVOLUTION?

Eco-efficiency

Until relatively recently there have been few challenges to the oft-stated view that free enterprise and market forces are an efficient mechanism for allocating resources efficiently and for meeting social and economic needs in the most timely manner. Conventional wisdom also has it that concerns for a healthy environment are important but must be balanced against the requirements of economic growth if a high standard of living is to be maintained.

During the past two hundred years plenty of evidence has been gathered to support this view. The Industrial Revolution occurred when machines powered in the first place by water, coal and charcoal took over the work previously done by labourers and allowed production capabilities to expand exponentially. At first this may have caused unemployment, but increased production led to reduced prices, increased wages and demands for a wider range of products in other industries. This cycle ensured that, by and large, everyone in the developed world enjoyed the benefits of employment in an ever-expanding economy.

However, the historic industrial model is increasingly seen as having a fundamental weakness that is only now becoming apparent: the creation of value is perceived as a linear process in which natural resources are extracted, processed and sold on as products to make profit. The wastes from production processes, and ultimately the product itself, are returned for disposal from whence they came, i.e. the environment, usually in the form of landfill. Until relatively recently, economists and industrialists have viewed this cycle as being essentially eternal – there would always be enough money to find and extract resources and there would always be sufficient places to dispose of waste.

Actually, evidence that this model was flawed was available from the very beginning of the industrial era. In the UK the negative impact of the Industrial Revolution on the environment was felt almost immediately. Charles Dickens, for instance, was sufficiently moved by the evil condition of the country's urban water that he made it a recurrent and sobering theme in many of his novels. In the emerging United States, the teeming herds of buffalo that inhabited the Great Plains prior to the westwards migration of white settlers, and which had provided an infinite resource for the indigenous population of hunter-gatherers, passed into history when exposed to the rapacious appetite of an industrialised society. Today a similar fate is being meted out to the world's fish stocks and forests (Chapter 1).

In the final decades of the twentieth century, however, there was a growing, though by no means universal, acceptance that the market must acknowledge the finite nature of the resources upon which it depends. As we saw in Chapter 1, the late 1970s and 1980s witnessed a false dawn in this respect with the development of products presented as 'green' or 'environmentally friendly'. Although this period is remembered rather more for the cynical use of the environment as a marketing ploy than for bona fide improvements in environmental performance, it nevertheless witnessed the start of the movement of environmental issues to the centre of the political and economic stage.

Now twenty or so years after the emergence of 'green' marketing, technology exists that offers the potential for truly sustainable economies. Hawken, Lovins and Lovins have wriitten a series of books that culminate in their ground-breaking work *Natural Capitalism: The Next Industrial Revolution* (Earthscan 1999). They describe how today there is a veritable explosion of environmental thinking that offers the prospect of reconciling economic and ecological goals. At the heart of natural capitalism is the idea that it is possible to do more with less by increasing efficiency and reducing waste, so-called eco-efficiency.

Eco-efficiency describes incremental improvements in the use of materials or, put another way, doing more (and better) with less and at reduced cost. *Natural Capitalism* addresses mainstream markets, such as the automotive industry, the service industry, real estate and water, and demonstrates clearly that businesses are harnessing new technology that will enable them to forge a new, profitable and sustainable relationship with the environment.

New markets arising from environmental issues

Traditionally, business has viewed the environment in terms of cost and risk – the cost of regulation and the risk of prosecution or liability. Most companies still do, although there are signs, reflected for instance in the Dow Jones Sustainability Group Index (Chapter 6) that some have begun to see the environment as an opportunity. These have looked beyond regulatory compliance and have identified competitive advantage in environmental issues. Indeed, the UK Prime Minister, Tony Blair, described the environment as a business opportunity with a growing market for environmental goods and services worth $335 billion, as large as the world market for pharmaceuticals or aerospace (Speech to the Confederation of British Industry/Green Alliance Conference on the Environment, 24 October 2000). In a similar vein, BP's chief executive Lord Browne has said that the enlightened company increasingly recognised how there were good commercial reasons for being ahead of the pack when it came to issues to do with the environment. But what exactly are the business opportunities offered by the environment?

In another major speech on the environment, Tony Blair put rather more flesh on his earlier reference to the 'environmental market' (Speech made by to the World Wide Fund for Nature Conference, 6 March 2001). While it is not always prudent to assume there will be a nexus between forecasts by politicians and market trends, his words provide a fair indication of the size of just one sector of the UK environmental market – the renewable energy sector.

First though, as if to underline the uncertainties which beset any forecasts concerning future markets, it is worth noting the chasm which opened in the early months of 2001 between the UK position on climate change and the US position. Mr Blair was firmly on the side of the then recently published report on climate change by the IPCC. Recognising that the report was not universally accepted, he said that it would be 'irresponsible' to treat it as mere 'scaremongering', rather it represented the 'considered opinions of some of the world's finest scientists' (*ENDS Report* no. 314, March 2001, p. 11). He went on to describe the Kyoto process on reducing greenhouse gas emissions as a 'monument to global diplomacy'. That view, of course, contrasted starkly with that of President Bush of the United States, who described scientific knowledge about climate change as incomplete and gave notice that he was opposed to the Kyoto Protocol.

Mr Blair's views on the emerging technology and environment market, are that green technologies were on the verge of becoming one of the next waves in the knowledge economy revolution. He acknowledged that the role of government was to accelerate the development and adoption of new technologies until self-sustaining markets took over. Here is a list of measures that the UK government, which is by no means leading in this area, is taking to encourage and mobilise industry:

- The climate change levy (CCL) is aimed at stimulating industry to invest in green technologies, reduce energy consumption and cut costs. This is complemented by the Carbon Trust, which was planned to start in April 2001, and which will recycle £200 million of CCL receipts over the next two years to accelerate the take-up of cost-effective low-carbon technologies and get them on the market.
- Electricity suppliers will be required to generate at least 10% of their energy from renewable resources by 2010. Box 7.1 indicates the opportunities that exist in this segment of the renewables sector.
- A ten-year plan will invest in modernising the UK's transport infrastructure and thereby reduce congestion and reduce emissions and pollution.
- Energy efficiency in the domestic sector will be improved by an investment of £1 billion in the Home Energy Efficiency Scheme, which plans to provide more efficient sources of heating and better insulation to 800,000 households by 2004. The scheme will also

significantly benefit the domestic heating and insulation manufacturing and installation sectors.

- A modest £100 million will be made available to support development of renewable energy technology including photovoltaics.
  Although development of photovoltaic applications is muted in
  the UK currently, other countries are investing significantly in this
  area (Boxes 7.1 and 7.2).

Box 7.1
Danish industry harnesses windpower

Denmark serves approximately half the world market for wind
turbines for electricity generation (Danish Wind Turbine Manufacturers Association, January 2001). This represents a turnover of
about $1.5 billion out of a total market of £3 billion. From 1994 to
1999 the wind turbine industry has grown at 40% per year,
supported by funds from carbon taxes, and is expected to grow
at 20% per year between 2000 and 2010. In 1999 Danish wind
turbine companies supplied turbines with a rated capacity of
1,800 megawatts, which is equivalent to two large nuclear or
coal-fired power stations per year. The Danish labour market
has also benefited by 12,000 to 15,000 jobs from industry's profitable innovation to meet environmental needs. Denmark plans to
produce 16% of its electricity from wind power by 2016. Some
estimates suggest this figure will have climbed to 40–50% by
2030.

Box 7.2
Photovoltaics: home-grown electricity

Photovoltaics enable electricity to be produced when a junction of
dissimilar metals is exposed to sunlight. Typically, thin photovoltaic panels are employed as roof panels or windows and produce
electricity for their host building and often in sufficient quantities
to be exported to the grid. Germany plans to have 100,000 photovoltaic roofs by 2007 and Japan 70,000 by 2002.

There seems little doubt that the environment is acting as a spur to innovation, and for companies and investors prepared to take the risk there may be significant returns. The era of clean energy is now inevitable. The threat of climate change is sufficient to provide the impetus for some, but even those who doubt that mankind is influencing climate cannot ignore the steadily decreasing costs of renewable energy, which alone must hasten its arrival. At its 2000 meeting, the G8 summit of the world's leading industrial nations set up a renewable task force to recommend how renewable energy should be promoted around the world. Although the final report was not to hand as this book was written, it seems unlikely that it will not recommend a vast increase in renewable energy supply.

Neither the UK nor the US has established a significant renewables sector; however, the Germans, Scandinavians, Dutch and Japanese, backed by commitments from their governments, all have a strong manufacturing base to meet future demands. On the other hand, the UK, with its deregulated electricity industry and some of the best natural resources in Europe for the generation of green electricity, represents a significant opportunity for investors in this sector.

We have taken the energy sector as an example and considered it at some length. But the automotive industry is also experiencing the need to provide solutions to environmental problems. For many years the only advances in design were incremental, in response to social and environmental pressures. Now the new technology has matured sufficiently to enable vehicles to be powered by compressed natural gas, liquid petroleum gas, hydrogen, electricity and hybrid petrol/electric drive systems. Each of these alternatives to conventional petrol or diesel internal combustion engines offers either zero or reduced pollution as well as noise reduction and reduced reliance on non-renewable fuel resources. Think of it, future traffic jams could be clean and silent. They also offer the prospect of diversity of fuel supply as a means of reducing risk to national economies.

New markets arising from environmental regulation

Many would argue that the market can best meet the needs of shareholders and society at large without the burden of regulatory control. The market's track record on the environment is not particularly good and most countries have introduced environmental legislation to make businesses behave in accordance with societal needs. However, operating within strong national regulatory frameworks need not necessarily hamper business. In fact, meeting the requirements of stringent environmental regulation may leave companies with a competitive advantage over those operating under more relaxed regimes. Scania, Sweden's multinational truck manufacturer, is based in a country with some of the strictest environmental standards in the world. Scania believes that to a large extent these regulations drive change and that technological improvements to meet regulatory requirements result in competitive pay-offs (*Scania Environmental Report 2000*). Scania's environmental policy sets out its environmental ethos:

> As a global manufacturer and distributor of heavy commercial vehicles, engines and related services, Scania is committed to develop products that pollute less and consume less energy, raw materials and chemicals during their life cycle. In order to achieve this:

- we strive to maintain a lead in commercially applicable technologies
- we work well within legal demands and promote internationally harmonised, effective environmental requirements
- we prevent and continuously reduce the environmental impact through development of products, services and production processes
- we take the environmental aspects and objectives into account in our daily work
- we have an open and regular communication with our interest groups regarding our environmental work.

By this we contribute to economical and ecological advantages for our customers and for society. Proactive environmental work is therefore of vital importance to Scania.

Scania's approach to environmental performance is evident in almost every aspect of its business and, where appropriate, trends are recorded in its environmental annual report. Scania has strict supplier evaluation criteria which put environmental issues alongside traditional concerns such as financial stability. An indication of the company's success in managing its environmental impacts while achieving commercial success is that raw materials, chemicals and water used to manufacture each vehicle have gone down year by year.

ENVIRONMENTAL MANAGEMENT SYSTEMS

What is an environmental management system?

An environmental management system (EMS) is a system by which a company controls its activities, products and processes that cause, or could cause, an impact on the environment. Essentially, this approach is based on the management of 'cause and effect'. EMS can be formal and certified, such as the internationally recognised standard ISO 14001 and the European Eco-Management and Audit System (EMAS), both of which are discussed later in this chapter, or they can be informal and uncertified, such as an internal waste minimisation programme.

Although it is difficult to be precise about the origins of corporate EMS, it is generally accepted that the International Standards Organisation's ISO 14000 series of standards originated from the Uruguay round of the GATT negotiations and the 1992 United Nations Summit on the Environment in Rio de Janeiro (see Chapter 1). At this time there was a steady growth in interest in national and regional environmental standards which fitted well with the commitment to protection of the environment made at the Rio summit. However, a plethora of national standards threatened to undermine one of the premises of GATT – the reduction of non-tariff barriers to trade.

Against this background, business fought against the introduction of mandatory EMS, environmental auditing and reporting, and argued for self-regulation and benchmarking with the market providing the impetus for improvement in environmental performance. US business, with its concern for litigation based on environmental reporting, influenced the development outcome of ISO 14001, the environmental management standard. Hence the standard requires businesses only to make a commitment to continual improvement and compliance with legislation; it does not establish absolute requirements for performance and it does not make any requirement for reporting.

In the European Union, where environmental objectives are accorded a very high profile by the Single European Act and the Treaty of European Union (Chapter 3), the Eco-Management and Audit System (EMAS) goes considerably beyond the rather bland requirements of ISO 14001. While ISO 14001 can be employed as the management system element within EMAS, the European system also requires an independently verified and publicly available statement on environmental performance. Thus, organisations intending to implement EMAS must be comfortable with making public commitments regarding their environmental performance and, importantly, plans for improvement. Significantly, they must also be comfortable with the need to report publicly on their achievements in this area, whether good or bad.

EMS are related to quality management systems. They provide mechanisms to promote a systematic and cyclical process of continual improvement. As can be seen in Figure 7.1, the cycle is no different than any other management cycle. It begins with planning for a desired outcome (in an EMS the outcome will usually be expressed in terms of improved environmental performance) and

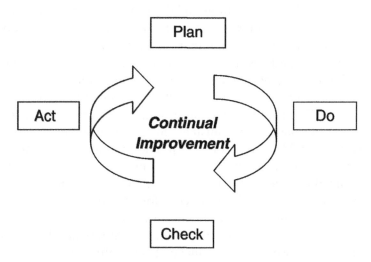

Figure 7.1. *Cycle of continual improvement*

moves on to implementation, checking to ensure the plan is working and, lastly, a review process based on observations made during checking. Amending the plan in light of the outcome of the process review completes the cycle.

Why should businesses implement EMS?

The are two complementary reasons for using EMS. First, improved environmental management is not only good for its own sake but a fundamental requirement for sustainable development. Secondly, environmental management is invariably beneficial for the bottom line and may become a pre-requisite for sustainable commerce.

It is increasingly evident that environmental issues affect business performance. For instance, poor environmental practices can lead to higher manufacturing costs, more waste, greater waste disposal costs, the expense of abatement technologies, fines for non-compliance with legislation, poor reputation and higher insurance premiums. While this is undoubtedly true, it is often maintained that any well-run business should address these issues routinely and can do so without recourse to an EMS. Curiously, the fact is that many businesses rarely examine their operations from an environmental perspective. Therefore one of the main business benefits of an EMS arises from the fact that it forces management to examine issues which traditionally were either overlooked or considered to be of little importance.

Energy consumption is a typical issue that is frequently overlooked or ignored. Surveys by the UK's Energy Efficiency Best Practice Programme in 2000 revealed that many companies had done little to improve energy efficiency in buildings, even though savings go straight to the bottom line. More than 400 businesses spanning the spectrum of energy use were surveyed. Only 37% of respondents believed there was a significant potential for cost savings. The report noted that the energy cost of buildings was often significant. For example, even for energy-intensive sectors such as light engineering, building costs, as opposed to process costs, could be 20% of a site's total energy consumption.

The report also recorded that only 30% of businesses had taken energy efficiency measures during the previous two years and that very few sites had specified energy efficiency measures during building refurbishment. It was acknowledged that part of the problem could be the relatively low cost of energy since the 1980s. On the other hand, as only 39% of businesses consulted knew how much energy their buildings consumed, it would appear that energy efficiency had simply been overlooked as a means to improve overall business efficiency. Given that energy consumption is an environmental issue, whether in relation to the unsustainable use of fossil fuels or to the emission of greenhouse gases, an EMS inevitably would require an assessment of its significance. Possibly for the first time managers would be presented with data that could identify opportunities to increase efficiency and reduce costs.

Before examining the business benefits of EMS in more detail, an examination of the basic requirements of ISO 14001 will indicate why an EMS can be such a powerful driver for overall business performance improvement. ISO 14001 is a cyclical system that can be broken down into the basic management actions of 'plan, do, check, act or review'. Figure 7.2 sets out the main elements of ISO 14001.

Although not part of the certifiable system, the guidance to ISO 14001 recommends that an environmental review be carried out as the first step in EMS implementation (an environmental review is a mandatory requirement of EMAS). Here are the items a typical review should cover:

- Identification of current and forthcoming legislative and regulatory requirements
- Identification of environmental aspects of a business (e.g. energy consumption) to enable those which have significant impacts or liabilities to be determined
- Evaluation of performance against specified criteria, e.g. shareholder expectations, sector best practice
- Feedback from incidents and legal non-compliances
- Stakeholder views
- Opportunities for competitive advantage

Following the initial environmental review, an organisation should fully understand its strengths and weaknesses with respect to the environment. More important, it should have identified the threats and business opportunities arising from environmental

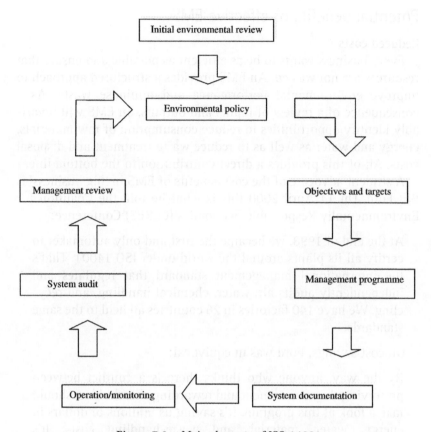

Figure 7.2. *Main elements of ISO 14001*

issues. With this information it can consider how to position itself to achieve competitive advantages. So far as business opportunities are concerned, the guidance for ISO 14004 stresses that an EMS offers the opportunity to link environmental objectives and targets with specific financial outcomes. In so doing, an EMS should ensure that resources are identified and targeted to provide bottom line and environmental benefits.

Potential benefits of effective EMS

Reduced costs

Every business wants to be as efficient as possible and ensure that resources are not wasted. An EMS provides a structured approach to improve environmental performance and minimise waste. As a consequence of a review of inputs and outputs, an EMS will invariably identify opportunities to reduce consumption of raw materials, energy and water as well as to reduce waste treatment and disposal costs. All of this provides a direct contribution to the bottom line.

A strident advocate of the cost benefits of EMS in 'big business' is Bill Ford. On 14 April 2000 this is what he told the Coalition for Environmentally Responsible Economies (CERES) Conference:

> At the end of 1998, we became the first and only automaker to certify all its plants around the world under ISO 14001. That's the international management standard that regulates and independently audits air, water, chemical handling, and recycling. We have 140 factories in 26 countries all held to the same standards.

On cost savings, Ford was unequivocal:

> By the way, anyone who thinks there is a conflict between preserving the environment and rewarding shareholders should take a look at this program. It's saving us millions of dollars in energy, water, material, and waste-handling costs. It's confirmed my strong belief that – in addition to being the right thing to do – preserving the environment is a competitive advantage and a major business opportunity.

Other examples of where companies have identified or made cost savings are described in Box 7.3. The Baxter case was chosen for two reasons. First, it demonstrates how big companies can make substantial savings by focusing on reducing their environmental impact. Secondly, Baxter was one of the first companies to realise that to have value, environmental management had to be accounted for as a mainstream activity. Even now, many EMS wither on the vine simply because they are not properly integrated with other management systems. Baxter recognised that the connections between environmental strategies and business performance are often not transparent or well understood within companies, let alone by financial officers. The company therefore pioneered the concept of an 'environmental financial statement' that not only quantified its environmental expenditure but also puts dollar values against the benefits (Baxter International's environmental financial statement at www.baxter.-com).

Box 7.3
Baxter International: a multinational company

Baxter International is one of the leading US healthcare businesses. It has 250 facilities worldwide and an annual turnover of about $7 billion and was recognised as one of Industry Week's 100 Best Managed Companies in 1997, 1999 and 2000. By the end of 2000 it had 36 sites worldwide, certified to ISO 14001 and planned to obtain ISO 14001 certification for all manufacturing, research and development plus other major operations by 2002.

Baxter's environmental financial statement (EFS) breaks costs into the 'basic programme', which includes environmental staff costs, auditor's fees and pollution control equipment and expenditure on remediation/clean-up and waste disposal. The most significant cost ($6.1 million) was for environmental staff, which totalled about 200 people worldwide.

Financial benefits were divided into savings, e.g. from waste disposal or energy efficiency, and income derived from schemes. The most significant of these were recycling ($5.5 million) and waste disposal ($3.0 million). Typically, for a company of Baxter's size, energy conservation made an important contribution too ($2.2 million). The net value of the environmental initiatives in 1999–2000 was $98 million. A basic breakdown of costs and savings for the period is shown below.

In the forward to its EFS, Baxter is unequivocal about the benefits of sound environmental management: 'Our experience makes a powerful bottom-line argument for environmentally responsible corporate behaviour that should appeal even to companies that haven't yet made environmental issues a priority.'

	$ million
Environmental costs	
Basic programme	15.0
Waste disposal	9.7
Packaging taxes	1.1
Remediation/clean-up costs	1.0
Total costs	**26.8**
Environmental savings/income	
Recycling income	5.5
Ozone depleters cost reductions	0.1
Waste disposal cost reductions	3.0
Energy conservation	2.2
Packaging cost reductions	0.9
Water conservation	0.3
Subtotal	12.0
Cost avoidance in 1999 from efforts initiated over the past six years	86.0
Total savings	**98.0**

Protection of current and future markets

ISO 14001 was launched in September 1996 and by the end of 1999, the last year for which figures were available at the time of writing, 14,106 certificates were held in 84 countries (ISO Survey of ISO 9000 and ISO 14000 Certificates, Ninth Cycle). This represents a quite significant rate of implementation, most of which has occurred in the Far East and Europe, where over 80% of certificates have been awarded. However, the figures for 1999 show that interest appears to be picking up in Australia and the US as well (Figure 7.3).

Quite clearly, as the take-up of ISO 14001 demonstrates, there is a growing pressure for companies to demonstrate good environmental performance. As a result, it is likely that some companies without an

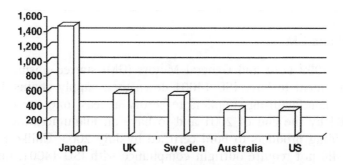

Figure 7.3. *New certificates: highest growth in 1999–2000*

EMS certified to a recognised standard may find that this becomes a barrier to trade. One of the factors likely to force the pace of implementation of ISO 14001 is the implicit requirement within the standard that organisations seeking certification should influence the environmental performance of their suppliers. Box 7.4 illustrates how this requirement is affecting the pace of implementation within the automotive industry and its supply chain.

But industry is not the only place where the presence of an EMS is likely to be a factor in gaining access to markets. In the UK there has been considerable debate as to whether government procurement policy should be used to promote the implementation of EMS among its vast number of suppliers. So far it appears that, although government departments are committed to implement EMS under the Greening Government initiative, there is little likelihood that they will be able to influence their procurement supply chains in such a direct manner as Ford and GM. Indeed, a note by the Treasury and DETR (predecessor to DEFRA) providing guidance on environmental issues in purchasing makes this very clear. The note states that it is not the UK Government's policy to require its suppliers to comply with EMAS or ISO 14001 as a condition of selection to tender or award of contract. It explains that such a condition could lead to higher prices by restricting those eligible to compete for orders and contracts and could conflict with EU rules on selecting providers.

Perhaps this rather perverse statement undermines the government's commitment to put the environment at the heart of its policy-making. However, the note is more positive when it goes on to state that it is permissible to ask suppliers to provide evidence

---

Box 7.4
Ford and GM

From 1999 Ford and General Motors (GM) started pushing the requirement to have ISO 14001 down their supply chains. Ford told manufacturing suppliers to certify at least one site to ISO 14001 by the end of 2001 and to have all manufacturing sites providing products to Ford certified by July 2003. Unlike Ford, GM did not require outright compliance with ISO 14001, rather suppliers were to implement EMS which were in conformance with ISO 14001 ('Steps towards sustainability', General Motors 1999/2000 report on economic, environmental and social performance). While GM's policy provided some flexibility for its suppliers, the company stated that third-party confirmation was strongly preferred although it would also accept a written declaration by a responsible executive that a site was operating an appropriate EMS. That said, GM let it be known that it would not take assurances as a matter of course and that suppliers would have to work hard to convince GM that their EMS were adequate (*ENDS Report*, no. 297, October 1999, p. 39).

The Ford and GM requirements were expected to boost uptake of the standard significantly. Ford estimated that about 5,000 of its suppliers would be affected while the GM requirement could affect as many as 10,000, although some suppliers would inevitably service both companies. Also, it would be reasonable to expect a domino effect further down the supply chain as suppliers impose similar requirements on their supply chains. The moves by Ford and GM reflect a general trend within the automotive industry. Rover and Jaguar (a Ford subsidiary) have already encouraged their suppliers to implement certified EMS, as has Volvo (another Ford subsidiary). Meanwhile, in the UK most motor manufacturing sites are certified to ISO 14001.

---

that they are able to operate an environmental management scheme where it is relevant to the contract. For example, it would be permissible to require an organisation seeking to provide facilities management services to be accredited or seeking accreditation to ISO 14001.

While this might seem to be a minor caveat, it is significant when it is considered that most of the vast collection of public buildings, offices and estates owned by UK central government and local authorities (the Ministry of Defence alone is the biggest landowner in the UK) are managed or serviced by contractors or, more recently, under public/private partnership arrangements. In light of this, it seems likely that possession of an EMS, and preferably certification to ISO 14001, will become an essential requirement within the UK facilities management sector.

Management of compliance with environmental legislation

An EMS provides a mechanism for continuous monitoring of developments in existing and emerging environmental legislation to enable management to assess compliance and take timely action based on accurate information. This is particularly important given that company directors can be personally liable for non-compliance and where penalties represent significant risks to individuals and businesses. An EMS does not guarantee compliance (see page 186); however, a good EMS operated with commitment should help management reduce the risk of non-compliance due to factors such as poor maintenance and inadequate training.

There is evidence that businesses with EMS will benefit from reduced oversight by regulators. In the UK the Environment Agency is a long-standing advocate of EMS as a means to control environmental risks and is committed to promoting their uptake by industry. However, until recently it had not taken account of their presence in its regulatory activities, much to the irritation of some sectors that would like to see a lighter regulatory touch in return for their EMS efforts. In March 1999 the Environment Agency started a research project to examine how EMS could be used to meet regulatory requirements and to explore the feasibility of coordinating EMS certification and regulation activities to the benefit of industry and regulator. Industry would feel a lightening of the regulatory load and regulators would be able to concentrate their resources on the less responsible or more risky end of the business spectrum. A similar project is under way in the US state of Wisconsin (Box 7.5).

Box 7.5
Wisconsin's Green Tier

On 20 February 2001 Governor Scott McCallum made a commitment to continue Wisconsin's Green Tier initiative. This aimed to 'strengthen the partnerships between businesses and the Department of Natural Resources... and provide for a more effective level of environmental management'.

The Green Tier initiative was started in 1999 and aims to examine new and innovative environmental regulatory approaches as a means of ensuring continued environmental protection and economic success. The trial is based on a 'regulatory choice' system in which organisations may choose to remain in a 'control tier', where they will continue to be regulated in the traditional heavy-handed manner and where compliance is assured by enforcement and fear of penalties.

This approach is labour-intensive for regulators and provides no encouragement for businesses to improve their environmental performance or to tackle non-regulated environmental problems. Businesses willing to meet certain conditions, among them the requirement to implement a 'compliance EMS', will be allowed to work their way out of the control tier into the green tier. In return for a lighter regulatory burden, businesses in the green tier will be required to go beyond mere compliance with legislation and implement a 'continuous improvement EMS'.

Wisconsin's Green Tier model envisages a 'carrot and stick' dynamic that will push or attract businesses into the green tier. The stick will be fear of non-compliance, enforcement and penalties as well as lack of competitiveness compared to equivalents in the green tier. In addition to enhanced competitiveness, the better environmental performance of green tier businesses will be rewarded lower insurance rates, greater share value and a better relationship with regulators.

Due diligence: banks and other lenders
Before proceeding with a loan to a business, clearing banks have a

duty to ensure that adequate security for the loan exists, that the borrower has the resources to meet all its liabilities and that the lender will not become exposed to liability associated with any security taken. To meet these responsibilities, lenders frequently include an environmental due diligence survey as part of the pre-loan investigation.

Environmental problems can affect lenders directly or indirectly. Typically, a lender may become directly liable should it become necessary to enforce its security by becoming a mortgagee in possession or to foreclose. However there is a limited saving provision for lenders under the Contaminated Land Regulations 2000 in respect of contaminated land, although there is always the possibility that the lender would become the logical target for claims in other instances. A lender could also be directly liable without realising his security if he had exercised some management control over the borrower's business.

Turning to the indirect impact of environmental problems on a lender, it is quite possible that the presence of contamination or pollution could adversely affect a borrower's business. This could result in the value of the security being significantly reduced and the need for action by the lender. Box 7.6 gives an example of how poor environmental management could affect a business's ability to trade.

Box 7.6
Total Oil and fuel distributor fined for groundwater pollution

On 1 February 1999 a pumping station at the UK Nestlé factory at Ashbourne, Derbyshire, was found to be flooded with kerosene (*ENDS Report*, no. 313, February 2001, pp. 55). The source of the kerosene was traced to a neighbouring oil products depot owned by Halso Petroleum, an accredited fuel distributor for Total Oil Great Britain. About 12,000 litres of fuel had overflowed when a Total tanker had overfilled a tank during a delivery a few days previously. The tank had no high-level alarm and no bund around it, although the Environment Agency had been pressing for the bund for several years.

Neither Halso not Total reported the spill to the Environment Agency. Clean-up was inevitably an expensive business and Nestlé had to suspend production for several days as a precaution

---

while checks were carried out to ensure its site boreholes were not contaminated. Charges were brought against Halso and Total and the case was eventually heard in the Crown Court, where both companies pleaded guilty. Halso also pleaded that its finances were fragile. Halso was fined a total of nearly £59,000 and Total £142,000.

After the hearing, the Environment Agency stated that the convictions sent a clear message to all delivery companies, as well as oil and chemical storage sites, that safe delivery procedures and spill containment measures were essential. Prevention would have been much cheaper than cure. This case was a classic example of where the presence of an EMS would have ensured as far as possible that the risk and consequence of spillage were identified and mitigated.

Environmental due diligence surveys have therefore become an essential feature of the screening process for lenders. The process endeavours to identify and quantify existing risks and to reduce the potential for future liabilities. Existing risks can be quantified by standard investigative techniques such as archive searches and on-site investigations. However, environmental due diligence surveys often point to the need for the lender to include an undertaking requiring the borrower to reduce the risk of future direct lender liability. Banks regard an EMS as an indicator of good environmental performance and as well-proven means to identify incipient problems (before they escalate to become liability issues) and reduce overall risk.

From a borrower's perspective an EMS can be used to demonstrate responsible behaviour. For instance, a good EMS will require a regular audit programme with results documented and assessed at management reviews. It would also record the fact that the organisation had learned and applied the lessons derived from incidents and accidents. Importantly, too, an EMS would go some way to proving that an organisation had a good understanding of compliance issues and was reasonably forward-looking regarding the potential impact of developments in environmental legislation and national policy.

Insurance: risk management and reduced liabilities

Insurance companies have become very restrictive, for obvious reasons, about providing cover for gradual pollution, e.g. pollution of underground water discovered only years after the onset of pollution, or pollution arising from the accumulation of small quantities of contaminant over a long period. However, it is still possible to purchase insurance to cover sudden and accidental pollution caused by 'identifiable perils' such as the failure of machinery or the rupture of pipework. In such cases the operational control procedures, e.g. maintenance programmes for critical plant, and contingency/emergency plans required by an effective EMS should lead to reduced environmental liabilities through improved risk management. It follows, therefore, that insurers are more likely to provide cover for businesses that have been certified to environmental standards such as ISO 14001. Moreover, it also follows that businesses with certified EMS will be able to demonstrate sound environmental practices and achieve lower insurance premiums than equivalent businesses without EMS.

Improved image and relations

A business's commitment to environmental improvement through its EMS can send very positive signals to its stakeholders at large and to local communities and environmental groups in particular. Many manufacturing businesses in, for instance, the chemical and engineering industries produce emissions such as smells, dust and noise that are often a source of irritation to surrounding communities. In some cases this reflects poorly on the business in the local press; in others it has been the catalyst to mobilise public opinion against planning applications for new buildings or to changes in processes. On the other hand, while the presence of an EMS underpinned by a robust commitment by senior management may not be a cure for all environmental ills, it provides evidence of good intentions. Moreover, an EMS provides a mechanism to explain publicly why and how a business is improving its performance. For example, the identification and implementation of training and procedures (including emergency procedures) for personnel involved in sensitive operations, should reduce opportunities for incidents or accidents which are often rightly regarded as a nuisance and, worse, avoidable by nearby residents.

EMS: what do they say about performance?

When the two main environmental management standards, ISO 14001 and EMAS, were launched in the mid 1990s there were high hopes that there would be a change in the relationship between regulators and business, which had been based on control exercised through regulation to a more mature arrangement. In this situation compliance would become the bottom line in environmental performance and the regulatory framework would act as a safety net to protect the environment from the activities of poor performers. Meanwhile, business would be able to move beyond mere compliance and take advantage of the commercial opportunities offered by improved environmental performance.

That said, not everyone was happy with the two standards. Many said that ISO 14001 had been so watered down as to be almost meaningless. After all, it was deliberately vague on how businesses were to demonstrate continual improvement; it contained no requirement for public reporting of performance and required only a 'commitment' to comply with legislation. On the other hand, although EMAS provided the rigour which many found to be lacking in ISO 14001, it seemed clear from the outset that few businesses would adopt it when ISO 14001 offered just as many commercial advantages for, some would say, much less commitment to improved environmental performance.

Few initiatives as novel and all-embracing as ISO 14001 and EMAS could expect to weather the early years of operational service without flaws appearing and without providing ammunition to their detractors. And so it has been, particularly with ISO 14001. Sceptics will point to incidents at the BP facilities at Grangemouth, Coryton and Sullom Voe (Chapter 3). Each of these sites was certified to ISO 14001 or EMAS and each was investigated as a result of pollution incidents and accidents. Other examples could be cited against certified companies around the world. Regulators, too, have expressed reservations about certain aspects of ISO 14001.

One of the lessons to emerge from the early stages of the Wisconsin Green Tier project (Box 7.5) is that ISO 14001 needed to provide tougher requirements on compliance, reporting and pollution prevention. Similar comments were expressed by the UK Environment Agency in its trial to assess whether the regulatory load could be lightened (*ENDS Report*, no. 309, October 2000, pp. 19–24). Other criticisms have concerned manufacturers' apparent unwillingness to address product life cycle issues and the fact that the presence of an EMS does not necessarily result in improved overall environmental performance.

Studies have been undertaken in Sweden and the UK to determine whether EMS make a difference to environmental performance. Neither study was able to state unequivocally that they did. It is difficult to say whether this was due to the fact that EMS had been in place for a relatively short time, which allowed too little time for the environmental 'culture' to grow, or whether the focus had been on compliance rather than performance improvement. In the US the Environmental Protection Agency (EPA) and state governments are funding work to provide further data in this area. (Information on studies into EMS performance can be found at www.environmental-performance.org and www.eli.org/isopilots.htm.)

Criticism of ISO 14001

One of the most common criticisms levelled at ISO 14001 is that it provides little or no focus on environmental performance. It has also been said that a full-blown EMS is too much for most SMEs, who have neither the management time nor the funds to implement a certified system. In response ISO launched ISO 14031 to provide simple guidelines for environmental performance evaluation. ISO 14031 is not a management system and for that reason it cannot be certified; it is a process to guide management in setting environmental performance criteria and assessing performance against them.

COMMUNICATING BETWEEN COMPANIES AND INVESTORS

Few companies identify how protecting the environment benefits their bottom line (Box 7.3). Perhaps this is because few environmental managers know how to speak to their accounting colleagues, and vice versa, or even know where to find them. While this is undoubt-edly a somewhat frivolous suggestion and far from the truth in most organisations, one would not think so from reading the content of many annual environmental reports. Most of these record 'tons or tonnes of waste reduced' or 'kilowatts of energy saved'. This is fine from a purely environmental perspective but businesses do not exist in a world defined only by environmental values. Banks and other lenders generally focus on a company's liabilities, such as expendi-tures needed to meet regulatory requirements, rather than on improved environmental performance, especially when performance is expressed only in environmental terms. Insurance companies, too, need to translate improvements in environmental performance into a measure of risk reduction that they can employ to increase or reduce premiums.

Analysts and investors need to penetrate beneath the environmen-tal annual report's record of environmental performance to assess risk, among other things. However, while environmental reports generally provide plenty of environmental information, it is frequently impossible to grasp their significance in financial terms. This may not necessarily damn a company in the eyes of a potential investor, but it might raise queries about the company's environ-mental performance and the commitment of senior management to EMS and other environmental programmes.

On the other hand, it seems fair to assume that the presence of detailed environmental accounts will strongly suggest that committed managers make accurate and pertinent environmental decisions in full knowledge of the consequences for overall business performance. Also, companies that employ environmental account-ing are far more likely to be able to identify and take advantage of opportunities to amend their activities in a cost-effective way. The benefits of environmental accounting are set out in Box 7.7. That said, few companies have fully integrated environmental accounts into their main financial accounts, but as the environmental agenda assumes greater importance and leading-edge businesses begin to think in terms of sustainability, there is a compelling need to put a price on environmental impacts.

Box 7.7
Benefits of environmental management accounting[1]

- Many environmental costs can be significantly reduced or eliminated as a result of business decisions ranging from operational and housekeeping changes, to investment in 'greener' process technology, to redesign of process/products.
- Environmental costs (hence potential cost savings) may be obscured in overhead accounts or otherwise overlooked.
- Many companies have discovered that environmental costs can be offset by, for example, generating revenues through sale of waste by-products or transferable pollution allowances, or licensing of clean technologies.
- Better management of environmental costs can result in improved environmental performance plus significant benefits for human health as well as business success.
- Understanding the environmental costs and performance of processes and products can promote more accurate costing and pricing of products and can aid companies in the design of more environmentally preferable processes and services for the future.
- Competitive advantage with customers can result from processes, products and services that can be demonstrated to be environmentally preferred.
- Accounting for environmental costs and performance can support a company' s development of an overall EMS.

[1] Source: US EPA Primer on Environmental Accounting 1995

One of the catalysts for change in the UK is Forum for the Future's Sustainable Economy Programme (*Green Futures*, March/April 2001, pp. 60–61). The programme aims to enable companies to put cash figures against the environmental impacts that already appear in many of their environmental reports. Companies such as the European arm of Interface, the leading US carpet manufacturer, Anglia and Wessex Water, and Bulmers have each participated in the programme. Ultimately, this work should enable a 'sustainability cost' to be worked out which, when reduced to annual trends, will provide managers with an indication of the effectiveness of their actions and investors with an indication of progress (or otherwise) towards sustainability.

CONCLUSION

The environment, while still a source of risk and liability, seems set to offer business an array of opportunities and possibilities undreamed of only a few years ago. No longer will mankind need to rely only on fossil fuels for his energy needs. Mature, operational renewable energy technology is here now and making money for innovative businesses supported by enlightened governments. Although the internal combustion engine is still king of the road, all the players are in place to topple it from the pedestal it has occupied for just over a hundred years.

True, there is a large measure of inertia to be overcome before new technologies can really begin to make themselves felt. For instance, one of the authors remembers writing an article extolling the virtues of compressed natural gas (CNG) for the CNG arm of an oil company only to be told that head office would not approve the piece as their prime business was oil not gas. Also, there are significant investments in the extraction of fossil fuels and the infrastructure to get them to the consumer, so change will not happen overnight. On the other hand, the investment opportunities are significant for those willing to take the risk in the new technologies. Not since the turn of the 1900s and the dawn of the motor car, domestic electricity and pharmaceuticals has such a vast range of investment opportunities been available.

But what of existing businesses; how can investors or analysts separate good environmental performers from bad? One indicator of good intent is the presence of an EMS. A good EMS will say much about the business values of a company. It will indicate one or more of several largely positive things. At one end of the spectrum, an EMS shows that a business cares about compliance and minimising the risk of non-compliance. At the other end, an EMS can indicate that a business is determined to go beyond mere compliance and reduce its environmental impact and costs. Either way, a good EMS needs top-level commitment. Without it the beneficial effect of the system quickly diminishes.

Much has been written about the beneficial effects of EMS, although with so few companies able to provide meaningful environmental reports, there is little evidence to convince the sceptics. On the other hand, environmental reporting is at last receiving the attention it deserves and there is reason to hope that before too long it will be possible to assess performance quantitatively from outside the company.

CHAPTER 8

SMEs and the Environment

INTRODUCTION

We have thus far focussed on larger businesses, their impact on the environment and the opportunities available for them. However it should not be forgotten that the overwhelming number of businesses are small and it would be wrong to exclude them from this discussion. Accordingly in this chapter we present the problems, or some of them, faced by companies and businesses at the smaller end of the business spectrum. Some public companies, among them the companies we have looked at in this book, have the will, the budget and the ability to deal with environmental issues and sometimes in addition the desire to publish the result of their efforts. With small or medium-sized enterprises (SMEs) the position is very different. If one assumes that the average annual turnover of a SME is $750,000 and that 0.5% is a reasonable percentage of turnover for an environmental budget then it is easy to see why the environment poses such a difficulty for these businesses.[1] Moreover, if the SME is faced with the weekly choice of meeting the wages bill or spending on environmental improvement, then there can be no question as to the order of priority.

[1] The EU published a report in May 2001 written by WRc plc and entitled 'Study on investment and employment related to EU policy or air, water and waste'. The study found that the cost of compliance with certain key directives EU-wide is €40 billion per annum, representing 0.5% of the gross domestic product of the 15 member states. It seems therefore not unreasonable to take a similar percentage figure for the purpose of this argument, although in reality it is likely that the SME budget for such matters is even smaller than 0.5%.

But before addressing the particular problems faced by SMEs and indeed caused by them, it is first necessary to understand what is meant by the term 'small or medium-sized enterprise' or as they are sometimes known 'small and medium-sized enterprises'. The authors prefer the former definition because, as will be seen, the SME sector is wide and diverse and to put small and medium-sized enterprises together serves only to obfuscate. There are a number of assumptions invariably made with respect to SMEs, but the sector spans businesses ranging from small specialists excellent at their craft and perhaps highly profitable, to those scratching a living in environmentally unacceptable circumstances. And there are, unsurprisingly, a number of legal definitions, brought into existence for a number of different purposes. It is therefore prudent to start with a review of some them.

DEFINITIONS OF AN SME

The EU differentiates between small enterprises and medium-sized enterprises.

A medium sized enterprise is defined as:

- Having fewer than 250 employees and either
- An annual turnover not exceeding €40 million ($34.3 million) or
- An annual balance sheet total not exceeding €27 million ($23.15 million) and
- An independent enterprise, in which not more than 25% of its capital or voting rights are owned by a larger enterprise

A small enterprise:

- Has fewer than 50 employees
- An annual turnover not exceeding €7 million ($6 million) or
- An annual balance sheet total not exceeding €5 million ($4.3 million)
- Is an independent enterprise as defined above

One English law definition (used to determine whether or not a company must file full accounts with the Registrar of Companies) is to be found in the Companies Act 1985. This provides that to qualify as a small company at least two of the following conditions must be met:

- Annual turnover must be £2,800,000 ($3.92 million) or less
- The balance sheet total must be £1,400,000 ($1.96 million) or less
- The average number of employees must be 50 or fewer

To be a medium-sized company, at least two of the following conditions must be met:

- Annual turnover must be £11,200,000 ($15.68 million) or less
- The balance sheet total must be £5,600,000 ($7.84 million) or less
- The average number of employees must be 250 or fewer

It will be noted that this definition is very similar to that adopted by the EU some ten years later.

There is no single definition of an SME in Canada either. This is because there is little agreement among interested parties about a definition. It is said that it is difficult to compare businesses in diverse sectors and there are so many data sets that it is difficult to get a clear picture of what characterises a small business.

One definition uses employment as a measure. Statistics Canada, for example, defines non-service and manufacturing small businesses as those with fewer than 100 employees, medium-sized businesses as those with 100 to 499 employees, and large businesses as those with 500 employees or more.

Statistics Canada classifies businesses in the service industry as small when they have fewer than 50 employees, medium-sized when they have 50 to 299 employees, and large when they have more than 300 employees. There is also a subcategory of small business, commonly know as microbusiness, which is reserved for establishments with fewer than 10 employees.

A second definition uses sales volumes. Revenue Canada, for example, defines small businesses as those with annual sales of less than $5 million, medium-sized businesses as those with annual sales of between $5 million and $50 milion, and large businesses as those with annual sales of $50 million. This measurement, however, is being used less and less for determining a company's size.

Lastly, to demonstrate the difficulty in defining an SME, the Organisation for Economic Cooperation and Development (OECD) has said:

There is no official or universally accepted definition of an SME. The definitions used vary widely among countries, but they are most often based on employment. In general, an SME is considered to have fewer than 500 employees, although many countries use a lower cut-off, say 300 or 100 employees. Some countries differentiate between manufacturing and services SMEs; in this case, services SMEs are usually defined as smaller than manufacturing SMEs. Some countries distinguish between autonomous SMEs and those that are connected to a larger enterprise or group, or identify an SME in terms of management structure (personal involvement of the owner or family-owned, for example). Finally, statistical definitions of SMEs often differ from those used for policy implementation purposes; for example, although a firm with 600 employees may not be regarded as an SME for statistical purposes, it may still be able to gain access to public support programmes designed for SMEs. (OECD SME website, 2001)

All that can be gleaned from this statement is that the main feature of an SME is that it is 'not large', in the sense that an SME is not in the core of the largest 10% or 20% of firms in that market or industry. This leads to a rough convention for categorising SMEs by numbers of employees:

Micro	1–4
Very small	5–19
Small	20–99
Medium	100–500

Having arrived at the conclusion that it is fruitless to seek a common definition, the next question to address is why it is that such a definition is necessary in the first place. The answer to this lies in the number of SMEs worldwide, however they are defined, and thus the impact they have on the environment. It should also be noted that SMEs are attracting increased attention in recognition of their economic role and their contribution to growth, but not unnaturally it is difficult to obtain an accurate estimate of the number of SMEs since such estimate must depend on the definition of an SME adopted.

According to the OECD, SMEs represent over 95% of enterprises in most OECD countries, generate a substantial share of GDP and account for well over half of private sector employment. A random review of available statistics reveals that in Canada in the past two decades, the number of new small businesses has dramatically increased and that the small business sector is responsible for more than 80% of employment growth in the past ten years. Of all established businesses in Canada, 78% have fewer than 5 employees, 97.6% have fewer than 49 employees and almost 99% have fewer than 100 employees. According to Statistics Canada, only 2,337 establishments in Canada have more than 500 employees. In Australia more than 90% of all businesses are claimed to be small businesses and they employ over half the Australian workforce.

The European Commission in their Staff Working Paper Report on the Implementation of the Action Plan to Promote Entrepreneurship and Competitiveness, published in October 2000, state that the EU average number of employees in SMEs is 66%. But it gives no indication as to the total number of SMEs in the EU or the percentage that SMEs bear to other businesses. Among the individual member countries, Belgium asserts that in 1997 (the latest date for which statistics are available), 69.0% of corporate employees were employed by SMEs and in Denmark the number of persons employed in SMEs in 1997 made up 68.7% of the total number of people employed in enterprises. In the UK it is reported by the DTI (Tables 8.1 and 8.2) that 2 million of the 3.7 million UK businesses are not incorporated, and 94% of all businesses employ less than 10 people (*The Environmentalist*, April 2001, pp. 30–31). Figure 8.1 shows the most recent available breakdown. And according to a 1998 study (A. Smith and R. Kemp, *Small Firms and the Environment: A Groundwork Report*, Groundwork Foundation, Birmingham), 99% of all UK businesses are small firms and they make up 58% of the workforce – more than half.

This admixture of statistics may be used to demonstrate one fact: there is no basis for comparison on a country-by-country basis. The EU surveyed member countries recently in an attempt to quantify the environmental risks posed by SMEs. Although the response to the survey was disappointing – only six countries responded – those responses show that it is still the case that relatively little is known

Table 8.1 *UK SME share of business, employment and turnover by industry at start 1999*

	Businesses		Employment		Turnover[a]
	Total number	SME share (%)	Total (000s)	SME share (%)	SME share (%)
All industries[a]	3,676,940	99.8	21,746	55.4	51.0
Agriculture, forestry and fishing	185,305	100.0	452	97.6	97.6
Mining and quarrying	3,860	98.4	83	30.8	29.4
Manufacturing	332,070	99.2	4,334	49.6	35.6
Electricity, gas, water supply	325	86.9	139	2.6	6.9
Construction	683,530	100.0	1,524	83.7	69.8
Wholesale, retail and repairs	533,140	99.8	4,416	52.1	54.8
Hotels and restaurants	154,400	99.8	1,598	55.6	52.9
Transport, storage and communication	225,725	99.8	1,538	39.8	39.9
Financial intermediation	59,455	99.4	1,043	21.1	35.5
Real estate, business activities	800,515	99.9	3,146	69.6	73.1
Education	107,850	99.9	255	83.8	86.5
Health and social work	203,465	99.7	2,107	41.7	33.7
Other social / personal services	387,295	99.9	1,111	76.7	64.1

[a] Finance sector excluded from turnover

about the contribution of SMEs to pollution and waste in the EU. It is the EU view that there is a very considerable collective contribution (probably around 50% overall) – less than the 70% estimated by Ruth Hillary in her 1998 research.

Table 8.2 *Number of businesses, employment and turnover by size of enterprise at start of 1999*

	Number			Percentage		
Number of employees	Businesses	Employ-ment (000s)	Turnover excluding VAT[a] (£m)	Businesses	Employ-ment	Turnover
None	2,324,340	2,708	90,463	63.2	12.5	4.7
1–4	963,615	2,395	221,986	26.2	11.0	11.4
5–9	201,835	1,459	123,029	5.5	6.7	6.3
10–19	109,280	1,533	149,451	3.0	7.1	7.7
20–49	46,955	1,462	147,505	1.3	6.7	7.6
50–99	14,450	1,011	102,860	0.4	4.7	5.3
100–199	8,165	1,131	116,638	0.2	5.2	6.0
200–249	1,570	349	38,633	[b]	1.6	2.0
250–499	3,220	1,121	149,275	0.1	5.2	7.7
500 +	3,515	8,576	804,039	0.1	39.4	41.4
All	3,676,940	21,746	1,943,880	100.0	100.0	100.0
All with employees	1,352,600	19,038	1,853,417	36.8	87.5	95.3

[a] Finance sector turnover excluded from turnover totals
[b] Less than 0.5%

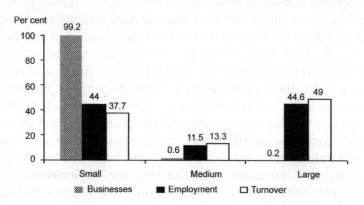

Figure 8.1 *Proportion of businesses, employment and turnover in small, medium and large firms at the start of 1999 Reproduced, with permission, from the UK DTI*

199

Some studies have been conducted (e.g. the Dutch TNO study, the UK Environment Agency study on waste and the recent Finnish study) and there are other methods, including the European Pollutant Emissions Register (for IPPC companies), which will provide more reliable statistics over time. If data collection were consolidated to include the data obtained from surveys such as the UK Environment Agency waste survey, the packaging waste returns, the air emissions data and data obtained from the application of economic instruments, reasonably accurate sector-wide estimates could be made of emissions from SMEs and non-IPPC companies.

So now, stripping out from the statistics the minority of SMEs that are profitable, law-abiding, environmentally at the cutting edge of technology and connected to the internet, the remainder are left which are variously described as causing between 50% and 70% of all pollution, having less access to the internet than the population at large, not cognizant of environmental issues and lacking the finance to deal with any matter other than the basics required for running a small business. This is of course a sweeping set of generalisations and indeed largely contrary in its view to the outcome of the OECD Bologna Conference held in 2000, which examined the status of SMEs with a view to promoting their future health and well-being.

One of the matters that came out of the meeting was that SME policies need to be tailored to the circumstances and priorities of individual countries and sectors, while contributing to sustainable development and social progress and the recognition that the work on SMEs by the OECD and other international institutions, encouraged continued multilateral exchange of experience and best-practice policies, thus strengthening partnership and cooperation among SMEs in OECD and non-OECD countries. In this context it is of course important that the regulatory environment does not impose undue burdens on SMEs and is conducive to entrepreneurship, innovation and growth through, among other things, promoting good governance and greater accountability in public administration; pursuing a fair and transparent competition policy, and implementing effective anti-corruption measures; and fostering the implementation of transparent, stable and non-discriminatory tax regimes (Bologna Charter on SME Policies 2000).

ENVIRONMENT: PERCEIVED ATTITUDES OF SMES

Pollution comes in many different forms, as emissions to air, to land and to water and as waste from processes and from packaging. Moreover, SMEs ignore the environment at their peril – environmental law relates to them as well as to all other businesses. But as noted earlier, SMEs do face particular problems.

Perhaps the most pressing is the need to run the business, which leaves little time for worrying about environmental issues. Unfortunately, this is a common problem but all businesses, whether SMEs or larger, do have an impact on the environment, be they industrial or service businesses. For every business uses and disposes of resources and products such as paper, water, and electronic and other equipment, and produces greenhouse gases from energy used for heating, lighting and office equipment and from refrigerants. Business road transport accounts for almost 10% of total UK carbon dioxide emissions. Moreover, there are indirect effects such as staff travel to work and the use or disposal of products made or sold.

The next commonly faced problem is the application of environmental legislation to SMEs. Unfortunately, there are few specific allowances made for SMEs in terms of environmental legislation, most member states applying the same requirements for all companies. The UK and the Netherlands are among those who have taken the most flexible approach, giving consideration to sectoral and even company-specific economic issues. The UK Packaging Waste Regulations offer a good example in that they only apply to companies with a turnover of more than £2 million, hence they exclude many smaller SMEs. Moreover, in Europe the approach to plant and processes that requires consideration of the principles of 'best available techniques' makes some allowance for economic considerations, in that there is reference to the cost of implementation, by sector if not by company, hence they can be of benefit to weaker SMEs.

Moreover, in the UK the data-gathering requirements of the Packaging Waste Regulations have caused many companies to re-evaluate their packaging needs and practices, saving very considerable sums of money in the process. The Environmental Technology Best Practice Programme (ETBPP) has produced a large number of case studies demonstrating the benefits of packaging reduction and reuse.

There is no doubt that smaller SMEs do have difficulty meeting the requirements of regulations, having very limited resources, particularly in terms of time and money. ECOTEC in their report on SMEs and the environment completed for the EU in February 2000 found the following main barriers for SMEs, in terms of compliance and in terms of making environmental improvements in general:

- Lack of time or staff resources
- Lack of financial resources (for investments)
- Lack of understanding of environmental problems and risks
- Lack of understanding of the potential benefits of environmental improvements
- Economic short-termism (i.e. quick payback on investments)
- Lack of expertise or confidence
- Lack of access to appropriate information (e.g. through IT)
- The view of environmental activity as peripheral to the core busines
- Initiative fatigue or overload (related to lack of staff resources)

SMES AND ENVIRONMENTAL MANAGEMENT

Whereas there has been a steady adoption of formal environmental management systems within large businesses, the same cannot be said of businesses at the small and medium-sized end of the business spectrum. In fact, a UK Department of Trade and Industry study reported that only a quarter of ISO 14001 certifications and EMAS registrations were by SMEs (DTI, 1995, 'Evaluation of study reports on the barriers, opportunities and drivers for SMEs in the adoption of EMS'). There are various reasons for this but several common factors have been identified.

Although the SME sector is a varied one, encompassing businesses (on some definitions) of up to 500 employees, most quote cost as a factor which dissuades them from implementing an environmental management system (EMS). The concept has often been sold to small businesses as a means to save money and there is little doubt that this is true for large businesses, where 1% of turnover is regularly quoted as a typical saving (*The Environmentalist*, April 2001, pp. 30–31). However, given the relatively small turnover of an SME, 1% is unlikely to be an attractive saving once manpower costs and the cost of consultancy support have been taken into account. Indeed, many SMEs would argue that management time is unlikely to be available in the first place given that it is invariably focused on the daily grind of survival in a competitive market. In addition to cost, lack of awareness and training is also a factor militating against EMS implementation. Linked to lack of training, many SMEs see themselves as lacking the skills and knowledge needed to prepare the data necessary to start the EMS process. Finally, ISO 14001 is often perceived as too complicated for the small end of the business spectrum.

On the other hand, there are reasons why SMEs should be interested in developing a systematic approach to environmental management. For instance, in the UK the Business and Ecology Demonstration Project (BEDP), which provided SMEs in north-west England with free environmental advice, reported that SMEs' knowledge of environmental legislation was generally low (BEDP Report, National Centre for Business and Ecology, 1999). The BEDP report also noted that many SMEs avoided contact with regulators instead of working with them and making use of the guidance and help they could give.

In fact, the study concluded that unless they were facing imminent prosecution, certain SMEs preferred not to tackle pollution issues. This should be of some concern given that environmental legislation, in the EU at any rate, continues to become ever more comprehensive and extensive. This was reflected in a study carried out by Norwich Union, one of the UK's major insurers, and reported in the *Times* of 23 June 2001. The study noted that more than a million small businesses believed they were unwittingly breaking the law because they were unable to keep up to date with EU regulations. Many businesses said that they did not consider that complying with EU law was a priority. The Federation of Small Businesses was recorded as saying that failure to comply could be costly, with businesses incurring costs of up to £50,000.

In Chapter 7 we also saw how EMS requirements were being passed down the supply chain, particularly in the automotive industry. Returning to the question of whether SMEs can employ environmental management to make cost savings, the BEDP report provided evidence that significant savings could be achieved provided some support was available to help management focus on environmental issues. The project is described in Box 8.1 along with examples of some of the savings made.

Box 8.1   *The Business and Ecology Demonstration Project*

The Business and Ecology Demonstration Project (BEDP) provided SMEs advice with the aim of 'optimising competitiveness through improvements to environmental performance', The Co-operative Bank, the European Regional Development Fund, the BOC Foundation and the Environment Agency funded the project which was managed by the National Centre for Business and Ecology. Eligible companies had to employ no more than 250 people, have a turnover of less than £32 million, be less than 25% owned by another company and be involved in manufacturing or distribution but not retailing.

The project identified over £170,000 of annual savings across nine companies. Most of these came from changes to processes or use of new technologies. One company, Horwich Castings Ltd, which makes castings for the railway rolling stock, agricultural applications, vehicle and engineering industries, identified annual savings of £16,600 with a payback of 16 weeks by changing from a high-volume low-pressure paint spraying system to an electrostatic system. This would also reduce emissions to the atmosphere from the spraying process.

Other savings arose from waste minimisation and recycling. Plastenik Ltd, which manufactures plastic injection mouldings, identified savings of over £16,000 through waste compaction and switching to reusable packing materials. Finally, Benson Components Ltd identified potential savings of £6,000 per year from closer monitoring of its scrap metal generation, £3,250 per year from replacement of light fittings and £1,500 per year from compaction of waste.

The Co-operative Bank confirmed that the results clearly endorsed its conviction that sound environmental practice made good business sense, delivered cost savings and often new business opportunities, and impacted positively on the bottom line.

Although the BEDP report stresses the benefits to the bottom line available from environmental management, its overall conclusions regarding SMEs' attitude to environmental performance makes depressing reading. That said, the conclusion that SMEs are ill-informed on environmental legislation is perhaps not too surprising given the large number of SMEs and the small number of regulators to police their activities. Perhaps, too, the penalties for polluting offences have hitherto been low enough to persuade some that payment of a fine is probably cheaper than investing in pollution prevention measures. Either way, it seems likely that many SMEs are at best 'vulnerably compliant' with legislation. In other words, although they may well operate with the best of intentions, they may not be compliant with current legislation requirements. Equally likely, businesses that have not systematically assessed their operations from an environmental performance perspective may well be running high risks of pollution.

Mindful of the need of SMEs to have access to inexpensive and user-friendly advice, there are several sources of information available in the UK. The Department of Industry sponsors the Envirowise Programme (formerly known as the Environmental Technology Best Practice Programme), which offers free, independent and practical advice to business to reduce waste at source and to increase profits. The programme covers a wide range of industries and provides detailed best practice and benchmarking information. It also has a fast-track consultancy programme aimed at providing SMEs with free waste minimisation audits. Other organisations also offer help to SMEs. Business Link puts local businesses in touch with each other to share environmental problems and solutions. The Groundwork network provides on-site practical support to SMEs, and Reduce the Use maintains a website offering sound advice on a range of environmental issues, including regulatory issues.

ISO 14001 has drawn criticism for being too complex and expensive for SMEs; the standard is currently under review with a view to making it more acceptable to SMEs. This may well be an important step since one of the hidden benefits of an environmental management system is its overall benefit to a business's general organisation and efficiency, especially in energy efficiency and waste reduction. A more recent output from ISO may also prove to be of value to SMEs.

ISO 14031 provides a practical standard for environmental perfor-mance evaluation. It describes a methodology built around environ-mental indicators to assist organisations in measuring and describing their environmental performance. This process, in turn, offers the opportunity to improve environmental performance without recourse to a full-scale EMS.

CLIMATE CHANGE LEVY AND OTHER ISSUES

It is clear that environmental legislation has had a considerable impact on the way business is conducted. This affects SMEs, probably more than bigger businesses. Unlike bigger businesses, SMEs do not always have access to advice of the type and quality more readily available to public companies, hence there is little doubt that many feel the weight of regulation is almost intolerable. For instance, the climate change levy (CCL) introduced by the UK Finance Act 2000 imposes a charge on all businesses for all energy obtained from fossil fuels. Intended to aid the UK in achieving targets agreed within the Kyoto Protocol, the levy is a tax on the business use of energy, imposed on the supplier, but passed on to the consumer to the tune of 0.43 pence per kilowatt-hour (kWh) for electricity, 0.15 pence per kWh for gas, 1.17 pence per kWh for coal, and 0.96 pence per kWh for liquid petroleum gas (LPG). Energy suppliers are responsible for registration and payment and must apply the tax at the time of supply to the end consumer in industry, commerce and the public sector.

In the UK the levy is expected to raise around £1 billion revenue in its first year, and this will be returned to industry principally through a 0.3% reduction in employers' National Insurance contributions. However, £150 million is being allocated for support for energy efficiency and renewables throughout 2001/2002. Thus, the levy is designed to be revenue neutral, moving the burden of taxation to penalise those behaving in an environmentally unfriendly manner. It is said that an important part of the UK government's Climate Change Programme is in helping businesses adjust in order to remain compe-titive.

For those paying the tax, fuel and electricity bills are predicted to rise by around 10–15%, an increase that is intended to be sufficiently draconian to concentrate the minds of managers upon means of increasing energy efficiency and the purchase of energy from renewable sources. Studies by the UK government's Energy Efficiency Best Practice Programme have shown that most organisations can reduce their energy bills by up to 10–20%, predominantly through no-cost or low-cost measures. However, while this may be true for some businesses, there are energy-intensive industries that cannot reduce consumption so easily. For such industries the UK government has set up a process of CCL agreements, whereby there will be an 80% discount from the levy for sectors of industry that commit to challenging targets for improving energy efficiency or reductions in carbon emissions. These agreements are mainly being negotiated through trade associations.

For the smallest businesses, or those using the least amount of energy, there is a different form of relief. These businesses may be classified by Customs and Excise as domestic supplies, and therefore be exempt from the levy, under the same de minimis principle that is used to calculate VAT. Electricity supplied to consumers up to a maximum of 1,000 kWh per month (33 kWh per day) falls into this category, together with small quantities of coal or coke (up to 1 tonne), piped gas – 5 therms (145 kWh) per day, or 150 therms (4,397 kWh) per month – and liquefied petroleum gas (50 kg cylinders, or a tank capacity of 2 tonnes or less).

The problems demonstrated for SMEs are obvious. Firstly, they must determine whether their activities qualify as a 'business' use of energy. Secondly, if they are obligated to pay the levy, it is then necessary to ascertain whether their industry is termed 'energy-intensive' and if it is, whether there is a CCL agreement in force that will assist. Thirdly, if there is such an agreement, whether in fact the SME will be capable of meeting its targets in terms of energy reduction. Lastly, there are other schemes in force which may merit attention. For example, the Enhanced Capital Allowance Scheme is designed to support a number of technologies which meet the relevant energy efficiency criteria, including combined heat and power and materials for pipe insulation.

Further technologies could be added to the programme subject to certification and cost-effectiveness. The programme includes a £50 million fund which is being made available for energy efficiency and renewables in order to provide advice and audits to SMEs, promote the development of new sources of renewable energy, and to encourage the research, development and take-up of low-carbon technologies and energy-saving measures through a Carbon Trust. Since the introduction of CCL in April 2001, there has been considerable complaint from SMEs that the tax is disproportionately and adversely affecting business. However, there is as yet no statistical evidence to support these claims.

Another recent piece of UK legislation that is likely to have significant implications for SMEs, is the Pollution Prevention and Control Act 1999 and the associated Pollution Prevention and Control Regulations 2000. These will gradually replace the Integrated Pollution Control (IPC) regime introduced by the Environmental Protection Act 1990 and the Environmental Protection (Prescribed Processes and Substances) Regulations 1991 (as amended) with a more stringent concept known as Integrated Pollution Prevention and Control (IPPC). About 2000 businesses were regulated under IPC; however, under IPPC the regulatory net will cover about 7,000 businesses. Moreover, with the emphasis now on *prevention* as well as protection, the new regime will impose controls on raw materials, energy and water consumption and will place greater emphasis on waste, noise and vibration reduction.

As we have already seen, because IPPC originated in the European Union, controls aimed at standardising systems throughout the EU are being introduced through a series of key reference documents called BREFs. These will have a profound impact on industrial pollution control and will particularly affect SMEs. Under the original UK IPC regulations, business had to meet technical standards known as 'best available techniques not entailing excessive costs'. In the Pollution Precaution and Control Regulations (and this is reflected in the BREFs so far published) the standard is BAT – best available technology/technique – defined as the most effective and advanced technologies and practices to prevent or, where this is not possible, to reduce emissions. The word 'available' in BAT is further defined as techniques that are 'economically and technically viable'. It will be appreciated that the reference to cost has been weakened and therefore no longer has the same importance in deciding whether a technology is suitable. Eight brefs have been published so far, covering

208

the following sectors: cooling systems, ferrous metals processing, chlor-alkali, glassmaking, cement and lime, iron and steel, non-ferrous metals, and pulp and paper. As SMEs in industries requiring IPPC permits make their applications, they will have to comply with these new standards or be forced to cease trading.

However, the eventual significance of BREFs will depend on how national authorities interpret the margin of discretion granted them by the Directive. The documents do not set out emission limit values, for instance, and in theory do not prescribe particular processes. The BREF for the chlorine industry, already finalised, suggests that BAT is achievable with only one particular technique.

To some extent, the UK government has recognised the increasing regulatory burden being placed on business. The Regulatory Reform Act 2001 provides ministers with powers to reform primary legislation that has become irrelevant or overcomplex, or which simply does not strike the right balance between burdens and benefits. On 17 May 2000 the chairman of the Federation of Small Businesses, Ian Hanford, stated:

> This Bill significantly expands the existing power to remove regulatory burdens from business and others. The ability for a Bill to reform whole areas of regulation is crucial and we are particularly pleased with the fact that any new burden, as dictated by the Bill must be proportionate and must strike a fair balance between the public interest and the interests of the persons affected by the burden being created. We believe that the Bill will be useful in helping to reduce the overall burden on business.

There is little indication yet that SMEs are benefiting from a reduction in regulation, and it has to be said that sometimes what represents assistance for SMEs results in disbenefits for the environment. One matter is clear, however: the impact of legislation on SMEs is great and growing by the year. The weight of legislation does not assist in the smooth running of business and sometimes regulators are overzealous in their enforcement of environmental regulation against the very sector of industry that most needs assistance from regulators not penalisation for compliance failures.

ENVIRONMENTAL REPORTING AND ACCOUNTING

Earlier in this book we examined the reasons why companies choose to report environmentally. Those reasons hold good for SMEs. Of course, some industrial SMEs are already required to report information on specific, mainly toxic, emissions to the Environment Agency or other statutory authorities. However, all SMEs could produce a report on wider environmental impacts, risks and liabilities, and their strategies, targets and policies. Doing so can be particularly important to an SME since it will help the management of environmental impacts, improve performance, and minimise potential risks. Preparing an environmental report may also help address resource efficiency in a way that will improve competitiveness.

An environmental report will distinguish an SME from its competitors. Stakeholders such as insurers, bankers, regulators, customers and neighbours are all likely to react more positively to the SME that shows it is aware of its environmental issues and is managing them rather than ignoring them. Moreover, it is said that, particularly in small organisations, employees are likely to respond well to the issues raised by environmental reporting and to participate in efforts to minimise impacts on the environment. However, preparing and publishing an environmental report will have costs which will include the initial cost of establishing an environmental management system, publication and distribution costs (if indeed the SME decides formally to publish the report), the cost of specialist advice (although grants may be available for some of the work). If the environmental management system is a formal one, it may be necessary to employ external verifiers.

But of course the SME will probably have as its greatest concern that reporting will expose areas where it does not perform well. However, many admittedly leading companies from all sectors have chosen to report voluntarily. Many of these companies would argue that transparency can improve relations with stakeholders and reduce the chance of misunderstanding. The argument runs true with SMEs. As with all other issues, the SME must carry out a cost-benefit analysis, with the cost of reporting weighed against the costs of not reporting, which might include incurring the hidden costs of not managing issues such as energy use, materials use and waste; the increased costs of insurance (or worse the withdrawal of insurance cover due to poor environmental management); the increased cost of borrowing from bankers or other lending institutions because their risks are greater than they would be were a suitable system in place; potential loss of markets through poor environmental profile; and poor relations with regulators, local authorities, planning authorities and local communities.

There are several different ways an SME can report: through an environment section in the annual report and accounts (this method is more suitable for public companies whose report and accounts are published widely); by stand-alone hard-copy reports (which can be very simple in form and which simply highlight the issues to be addressed); or by stand-alone web-based reports (which are successfully employed by SMEs from time to time). Whichever form is adopted, there are certain important elements that should be included in the report:

- Environmental performance indicators, ie. key impacts setting targets for improvement
- A profile of the SME
- The SME's environmental policy
- A statement from the chief executive
- A description of the environmental management system
- A statement as to legal compliance and details of any fines over £1,000
- Supply chain issues

Of course it may not be possible to report fully in early years. In such cases it may be necessary to adopt a step-by-step approach. The areas where some SMEs may have difficulties include the gathering of reliable performance data, setting quantified targets and describing action taken to green supply chains. On balance, however, there can be little doubt that if the SME can find the time and the budget, an environmental report can be helpful in establishing the credibility of the organisation.

CONCLUSION

There are some problems that affect buinesses of all sizes; their nature is the same, only their scale is different. The real contrasts between SMEs and large public companies lie in budgetary concerns and management ability. This is not to say that all public companies are well run and have unlimited finance or that all SMEs are poorly managed and entirely lacking in an environmental budget. The truth, as always, lies between the two extremes. It is beyond doubt that SMEs are more stretched generally and thus face greater problems, most particularly with control systems. This is evidenced by the fact that more environmental prosecutions are of SMEs and their officers or managers than of public companies, and it remains a fact that in England there has been no successful personal prosecution of a director or manager of a public company for offences committed by his company.

Compliance issues are therefore of greatest importance in an environmental context. Contrary to their mistaken belief that they are too small to be noticed, regulators are well aware of SMEs and the danger they may pose to the environment. Although it is recognised both at OECD and EU level that regulation is cumbersome and difficult for SMEs, and not only in an environmental context, efforts to relax significantly the regulations as they apply to SMEs have so far signally failed. Of course, the contrary argument that pollution is caused more by SMEs than bigger organisations makes it difficult to support from an environmental standpoint the suggestion that there should be relaxation of regulation if the result is an increase in pollution.

However, the budgetary concerns faced by many SMEs and identified at the start of this chapter, mean there is limited scope for compliance and more. Part of the solution to this seemingly circular problem is making cheap finance or grants available to SMEs for environmental improvement. However, cheap finance from conventional sources, such as banks, may not always be available, particularly if the business cannot demonstrate a reasonable record in environmental performance. Moreover, grant applications are notoriously difficult to complete, and often do not provide a sufficiently large contribution to the cost of the work sought to be done.

So it is plain that improved environmental performance will not result solely from grants or loans. In the end, SMEs must accept that environmental improvement starts with management and that management may need first to seek external help, for example, in training and/or bespoke consultancy advice. Governments world-wide must ensure that SMEs are allowed to continue to trade, without being weighed down by legislation and too much regulation, yet controlled to ensure they do not contribute to pollution statistics.

CHAPTER 9

Final Thoughts

Two hundred years of industrial heritage have provided cheap food, inexpensive goods, cheap and plentiful energy, a great degree of employment and an increasingly good standard of living for much, but by no means all, of the world. But this has been achieved at a cost to the environment. Land has been contaminated, natural resources have been squandered and in some cases reduced to perilously low levels. Air quality in cities is a matter for concern and the water that surrounds our shores is polluted and bereft of fish stocks.

Individuals divide into countries (developed or undeveloped), their need or desire for material wealth, their recognition (or not) of environmental issues and their desire (or not) to see an improvement in the environment. Values should therefore be the driving force behind decision-making in corporate management. It is now beyond doubt that environmental issues have assumed a significance in corporate economic values, and protection of the environment has become an important goal for many individuals, for some companies and for society at large. This is reflected in increasing amounts of environmental regulation and legislation, and it is not without good reason that breach of environmental law is, in most countries, a criminal rather than a civil matter.

Through increased regulatory and stakeholder pressure and the growing cost of raw materials (including energy) companies have slowly begun to attend to problems of excessive use of energy and other natural resources and the issues surrounding waste reduction, minimisation, reuse and recycling. Progress on these matters is revealed largely through the gathering, tracking and disclosure of environmental information in company reports. But as has been seen, data is not always logically compiled and not always easy to understand and interpret. Indeed it is often very difficult to compare data within a single company from year to year, particularly if the underlying business of the company changes. And if it is hard to compare data used inside a single company, that is as nothing compared with the problems of assessing the value of information across an industry sector.

Benchmarking – setting targets, or benchmarks, to provide the standard against which actual performance can be measured – is used by internal and external stakeholders as a basis for future action and for further continual improvement. But benchmarking is not always helpful since the conditions from company to company, even in the same sector, may vary considerably. It should, however, be recalled that both the ISO 14000 series and EMAS provide benchmark information for site comparisons. More stretching threshold levels may be imposed in response to the expressed expectations of key external stakeholders, such as companies requiring a supplier to achieve certification to a recognised environmental management system standard.

Additionally, investors may impose ethical screening requirements on companies, forcing them to demonstrate that particular performance control measures are in place. Compliance plus – threshold levels which exceed those required by legislation – might also be imposed in response to internal information requirements, which are themselves a response to high-level corporate objectives. For example, many companies recognise that superior environmental performance is critical to their long-term success and have publicly committed themselves to achieving best practice or at least sectoral leadership on environmental management.

But data collection should not just be an exercise in itself. No company waits for the end of the financial year before determining its performance and reporting to its shareholders and regulators. Instead companies track the key elements of their financial performance internally on an ongoing basis, as a means of predicting their longer-term performance and maximising their control over that performance. The same should be true of environmental data collection. Not only must collection be centred on well-defined criteria, but it must be for specific reasons and to produce specific information. Knowledge creation means focusing on discrete issues and designing metrics to produce that knowledge in a meaningful way. To take a very simple example, if Company A reports that it sent 5,000 tonnes of waste to landfill in one year and 3,000 tonnes the following year, but fails in the same disclosure to mention that half the business was sold (which disguises the fact that waste creation had actually increased) then it is artless in the extreme.

To improve environmental performance, management must be informed about relevant environmentally induced financial impacts on the company as well as those created by the company. One of the mechanisms to achieve this is an environmental management system, designed to improve performance and capable of providing management information. Accounting is the central economic management information system, and for those companies that already have a quality system in place, that is the starting point for an environmental management system since both systems have some common features. The accounting system and the EMS between them form the basis for integrated planning and this is a core element in the corporate control system.

In this book we have sought to look at how environmental issues have started to shape financial accounting and reporting and what further issues companies must address to move from simple environmental recognition and improvement to total social responsibility. For this purpose the issues of accounting standard setting have been investigated, as have the different mechanisms for report writing. It is of some concern that with the passage of time there is an increasing number of accounting standards, some national and some international, and it is necessary to remark that this will not necessarily be helpful to the company, its advisers or its stakeholders.

From the viewpoint of the company, it needs to be sure the system it adopts will remain valid for some years. From the viewpoint of the company's professional advisers, they need to know that the standards selected will be adequate for the purpose and not subject to undue change From the viewpoint of the stakeholders, the fewer the choice of standards, the easier it is to understand what is being reported on and why. Moreover, an excess of accounting standards dealing with environmental issues will confuse the reader, waste the company's resources on accounting fees, and generate uncertainty on the bottom line effects, especially if different results can be achieved by using different standards. All of this of course means that the information, even if available, is very hard for the average audience to find and understand.

The purpose of environmental reporting and accounting must in the first place be to improve the access to and then the usefulness of information supplied to investors, regulators and other stakeholders. It has been noted that in different companies, different groups of stakeholders seem to have priority and that different companies approach the business of reporting and accounting in different ways. It is of course a fact that a relatively small number of companies report and account in a meaningful way, but also a fact that the number is growing and growing significantly.

Because of the difficulty in assessing the quality of the environmental information provided and because an increasing number of people wish to invest in socially responsible companies, a new industry has grown up to service their requirements. This new service industry weighs the environmental worth of companies and decides whether they are fit to be included as investments in 'green' funds. There is more than one way of carrying out the necessary information seeking, and weighted matrices play their part in the decision-making process. It is also plain that shareholder activism, so long a feature of the US company AGM, is finding its way across the Atlantic as has been seen recently with BP.

And we have seen too what happens when companies fall behind in the race for greater environmental performance. The public can and do make their collective displeasure known. The new global economy is characterised by previously unimaginable numbers of customers being wooed by a bewildering range of international corporations and their products. In this business environment, reputation has become a significant determinant for potential customers deciding which products or services to buy.

While brands proliferate and come and go, reputations are perhaps the single consistent feature which marks any company out from its competitors, no matter where it operates in the world. At one time, reputations were remarkably resilient despite variations in company performance and dips in customer satisfaction. Perhaps this was because many companies were not only household names but closely identified with nations, too. One only has to think of emblematic brand names such as Rolls-Royce, Harrods and Coca-Cola. Muted criticism might be acceptable but nobody would dream of acting with the intention of damaging the reputation of such companies. Not so today, when deference is long dead and many are apt to say the bigger they are, the harder they fall.

As the global economy has grown, so has access to information and cheap portable communications. The global population may not be any wiser than it once was but it is better informed and highly opinionated. Even more significant, where individuals are either simply unable or insufficiently motivated to take companies to task over economic policy, human rights or environmental issues, pressure groups have emerged to tap local resentment and articulate compelling and potentially ruinous arguments against even the mightiest corporations. Today, if companies declare themselves to be on the side of the environment, they had better have thought through what that means and ensure that practice is consistent with rhetoric. Reputations are no longer awarded for a lifetime. They will be frequently assailed and often from surprising directions. It is no longer sufficient to consign reputation to a glossy brochure for distribution when the going gets tough – it will already be too late by then. Reputations must be nurtured and refined to appeal to stakeholders who will rarely share the same view of any one organisation.

Reputation is gained and maintained by the systematic applications of corporate values into everyday operations, by effective communication of those values to staff and other stakeholders and by setting corporate goals, objectives and targets and providing the resources, training and personnel to achieve them. Above all, it is gained and maintained by integrating all of these to improve business performance.

So to return to the means by which a company can demonstrate its environmental performance, a potential solution is in the increasing use of environmental performance measurement. This is emerging as a critical component in managing wider business risks, irrespective of the extent to which a company must comply with legally imposed performance levels. While that is of course important, it is in some senses more important for the company to establish and maintain internal control over environmental performance because it is recognised as promoting superior business performance. Assistance in developing environmental performance indicators is available in the form of ISO 14031 *Guidance on environmental performance evaluation*. It defines three broad areas for measurement:

- *Environmental condition indicators*: information about the local, regional, national or global condition of the environment in which the company operates.
- *Operational performance indicators*: information about the environmental consequences of the company's operations, including those relating to inputs, physical processes and equipment, and outputs.
- *Management performance indicators*: information about the controls, including management systems, that are in place and the decisions and actions taken by management in response to them.

ISO 14031 also provides the means to express indicators for environmental performance evaluation (EPE). It suggests direct measures or calculations which provide the raw information and data; relative measures or calculations which interpret the basic information in relation to another parameter, such as production volumes; normalised and indexed information as required by the GRI, which compares direct or relative information with a stated baseline figure such as performance in the year in which measurement commenced; aggregated measures which collate information from a range of comparable sources, such as different facilities producing the same output; and weighted measures which take raw data or information and adjust it through the application of a factor or coefficient that reflects the relative significance of the information.

Earlier on we discussed the issues of risk. However, the potential of non-governmental organisations (NGOs) to create risk for companies should not be overlooked. Companies have received very public criticism from NGOs, for example, for leaving industrial inner cities, failing to ensure that suppliers apply human rights standards, and polluting the environment. Hardly an area of business remains unaffected by such pressures; from chocolate makers to oil refiners, all have received their share of criticism. And while the public exercise their own form of pressure, companies can actually enlist the support of NGOs to assist companies reduce risks associated with specific projects or general operations. This is not as dangerous a strategy as might at first appear, NGOs sometimes represent stakeholders outside the core corporate structure and can provide an early warning network of potential problems with corporate activities.

And finally, what of the environment as a business opportunity? Chapter 1 suggested that mankind's economic and social development would take place against the pollution legacy of two centuries of industrialisation, soaring population growth and increasingly limited natural resources. Although little in this world can be taken for granted, as President Bush's hostility to the Kyoto Protocol made abundantly clear, there seems little doubt that for those prepared to develop, market or invest in solutions to the world's environmental ills, the future offers many opportunities for business.

According to the UK's Department of Trade and Industry, the global market for environmental goods and services is currently estimated at $335 billion, comparable with the world markets for pharmaceuticals or aerospace, and is forecast to grow to $640 billion by 2010 (DTI White Paper, 2001, *Opportunity for all in a world of change*). The past fifty years or so have seen industries maintaining or enhancing their competitiveness by increasing labour productivity. This will continue to be an important factor in business. However, it seems likely that in future the strategies of leading businesses will also be characterised by their willingness to embrace eco-efficiency – doing more with fewer resources and minimum waste.

Bibliography

Azzone, G., Manzini, R. and Noci, G., Evolutionary trends in environmental reporting, *Business Strategy and the Environment*, 5(4) December 1996, 219–230.

Bartelmus, P., Bringezu, S. and Moll, S., *Dematerialization, Environmental Accounting and Resource Management*, EU, 1999.

Beardsley, D.H., The greening of small business, *The Environmentalist*, Magazine of the Institute of Environmental Management, April 2001.

Brown, L., Flavin, C. and French, H., *State of the World*, Earthscan, London, 1999 and 2000.

Brooks, I. and Weatherston, J., *The Business Environment, Financial Times*/Prentice-Hall, London, 2000.

Business and Ecology Demonstration Project Report, National Centre for Business and Ecology, 1999.

Cairncross, F., *Costing the Earth a Challenge for Governments, the Opportunities for Business*, Harvard Business School Press, Boston, MA, 1993.

Centre for Tomorrow's Company/KPMG, *Distortions and Deficiencies in Institutional Investment*, Evidence to the Myners Review of Institutional Investment, 2000.

Christie, I. and Rolfe, H., *Cleaner Production in Industry, Integrating Business Goals and Environmental Management*, Policy Studies Institute, London, 1995.

DTLR (formerly DETR): Waste Strategy 2000, IPPC Consultations, Contaminated Land Consultations, Sustainable Development Documents (all available at http://www.dltr.gov.uk).

Edwards, D., *The Link Between Company Environmental and Financial Performance*, Earthscan, London, 1998.

ENDS Report, Environmental Data Services Ltd., London

Evaluation of study reports on the barriers, opportunities and drivers for SMEs in the adoption of EMS, Department of Trade and Industry.

Freshfields, *Environmental Law*, Tolley, 2001.

Goyder, M., *Connected Economy – Disjointed Society* (SLIM Annual Lecture), Centre for Tomorrow's Company, London, 2000.

Green Government, Partnership Media Group Ltd.

Harvey, G., *The Killing of the Countryside*, Vintage, London, 1997.

Hawken, P., Lovins, A. and Lovins, L.H., *Natural Capitalism, the Next Industrial Revolution*, Earthscan, London, 1999.

Hillary, R., *Small and Medium Sized Enterprises and the Environment*, Greenleaf, Sheffield, 2000.

Howes, R., Skea, J. and Whelan, B., *Clean and Competitive*, Earthscan, London, 1997.

ICAEW, *Internal Control: Guidance for Directors on the Combined Code* (The Turnbull Report), ICAEW, 1999.

ILGRA, *Risk Communication: A Guide to Regulatory Practice*, HSE, 1998.

Inform, *Journal of the Institute of Risk Management*, December 2000.

The ISO Survey of ISO 9000 and ISO 14000 Certificates, Ninth Cycle, International Organization for Standards.

Korten, D.C., *When Corporations Rule the World*, Earthscan, London, 1995.

KPMG, *KPMG International Survey of Environmental Reporting*, 1999.

Lister, C., *European Environmental Law*, Wiley, New York, 1996.

Making a Corporate Commitment, UK Department of the Environment Transport and the Regions, 2000.

McIntosh, M., Leipziger, D., Jones, K. and Coleman, G., *Corporate Citizenship*, Pitman, London, 1998.

McIntosh, M. *Visions of Ethical Business*, Financial Times/Prentice-Hall, New York, 2000.

McLaren, D., Bullock, S. and Yousef, N., *Tomorrow's World*, Earthscan, London, 1998.

Patterson, W., *Transforming Electricity*, Earthscan, London, 1999.

Peters, G., *Waltzing with Raptors*, Wiley, New York, 1999.

Pollution Handbook 2001, National Society for Clean Air, 2000.

Romm, J., *Cool Companies*, Earthscan, London, 1999.

Sasseville, D.R., Wilson, G.W. and Lawson, R.W., *ISO 14000, Answer Book*, Wiley, New York, 1997.

Schaltegger, S. and Burritt, R., *Contemporary Environmental Accounting*, Greenleaf, Sheffield, 2000.

Roberts, H. and Robinson, G., *ISO 14001 EMS Implementation Handbook*, Butterworth Heinemann, London, 1998.

Spotlight on Business Environmental Performance, Environment Agency.

Symonds Group (United Kingdom) in association with Argus (Germany), Cowi Consulting Engineers and Planners (Denmark) and PRC Bouwcentrum (the Netherlands), *Construction and Demolition Waste Management Practices and their Economic Impacts*, EU, 2000.

Sustainability/UNEP Buried Treasure, 2000.

Thomas, A., Pettigrew, N., Hulusi, A. and Candy, S., *The Changing Role of the Occupational Scheme Trustee*, DSS Research Report 124, Leeds, 2000.

Von Weizsäcker, E., Lovins, A. and Lovins, L.H., *Factor Four*, Earthscan, London, 1997.

Wackernagel, M., *Advancing Sustainable Resource Management*, EU, 2001.

Warren, M.J., A Risk Analysis Model to reduce computer security risks among healthcare organisations, *Risk Management: An International Journal*, Vol. 3, No. 1, Perpetuity Press, 2001.

Welford, R. and Gouldson, A., *Environmental Management and Business Strategy*, Pitman, London, 1993.

White, Elements, *The Journal of the Environment Council*, March 2001.

WRc plc., *Study on Investment and Employment Related to EU Policy on Air Water and Waste*, EU, 2000.

de Zeeuw, A., *Resource Management. Do We Need Public Policy?*, EU, 2001.

Index

227

Printed and bound by CPI Group (UK) Ltd, Croydon, CR0 4YY

16/04/2025